CULTURE SHOCK!

Barcelona
At your Door

Mark Cramer

D1469157

Graphic Arts Center Publishing Company
Portland, Oregon

In the same series

Argentina	*France*	*Malaysia*	*Sweden*
Australia	*Germany*	*Mauritius*	*Switzerland*
Bolivia	*Greece*	*Mexico*	*Syria*
Borneo	*Hong Kong*	*Morocco*	*Taiwan*
Britain	*Hungary*	*Myanmar*	*Thailand*
Burma	*India*	*Nepal*	*Turkey*
California	*Indonesia*	*Netherlands*	*UAE*
Canada	*Iran*	*Norway*	*Ukraine*
Chile	*Ireland*	*Pakistan*	*USA*
China	*Israel*	*Philippines*	*USA—The South*
Cuba	*Italy*	*Singapore*	*Venezuela*
Czech Republic	*Japan*	*South Africa*	*Vietnam*
Denmark	*Korea*	*Spain*	
Egypt	*Laos*	*Sri Lanka*	

Barcelona At Your Door	*Paris At Your Door*	*Living and Working*
Chicago At Your Door	*Rome At Your Door*	*Abroad*
Havana At Your Door		*Working Holidays*
Jakarta At Your Door	*A Globe-Trotter's Guide*	*Abroad*
Kuala Lumpur, Malaysia	*A Parent's Guide*	
At Your Door	*A Student's Guide*	
London At Your Door	*A Traveller's Medical Guide*	
New York At Your Door	*A Wife's Guide*	

Illustrations by TRIGG

© 2001 Times Media Private Limited

This book is published by special
arrangement with Times Media Private Limited
Times Centre, 1 New Industrial Road, Singapore 536196
International Standard Book Number 1-55868-537-5
Library of Congress Catalog Number 00-102145
Graphic Arts Center Publishing Company
P.O. Box 10306 • Portland, Oregon 97296-0306 • (503) 226-2402

Printed in Singapore

to Bill Olmsted

A NOTE TO THE READER

Only the most strategic addresses and phone numbers are listed within the text. Anyone who arrives in Barcelona has access to easy-to-use directories. Prices, phone numbers and addresses can and will change, and any such information in these pages is intended as a head start for the larger goal of this book: to help the visitor adapt to and be enriched by Barcelona.

In Barcelona, without rhyme or reason, words appear in either Catalan or Spanish, or both. If you see this happening in this book, it simply represents the way bilingualism occurs in its natural Barcelona habitat.

ACKNOWLEDGMENTS

Barbara Hallé i Boix, for helping me with my Catalán and sharing her ideas on Barcelona; our old friends Luis Vega, Monse Arago and their daughters Neus and Adelaide, for gourmet experiences with Catalán food and the great conversation that came with it; Daniel Giordano Leis, for photos, ongoing exchange of ideas, and a great cup of coffee at his Terra Bar in Gràcia; Manuel Iglesias, for his spontaneous professional advice, and photos; Laura Salom and Mario Rubert, for their valuable time, through Barcelona Activa, in introducing me to the Barcelona business scene; Marcos Marín, waiter at Los Caracoles, for photos of the restaurant where he has worked for more than a decade; a city planning official in Sant Martí, for an insider's view of Barcelona's urban development; the librarians at the Centre d'Études Catalanes of La Sorbonne; the members of the Villa del Arte art collective, including María Cañellas and Nemo Jantzen, for supplying photos of their art; Kathy and Dave Smoley, for their generosity with ideas and photos; María Rosa Piulats, from City Hall, for more fine photos; and so many other people in Barcelona who helped me with this project.

CONTENTS

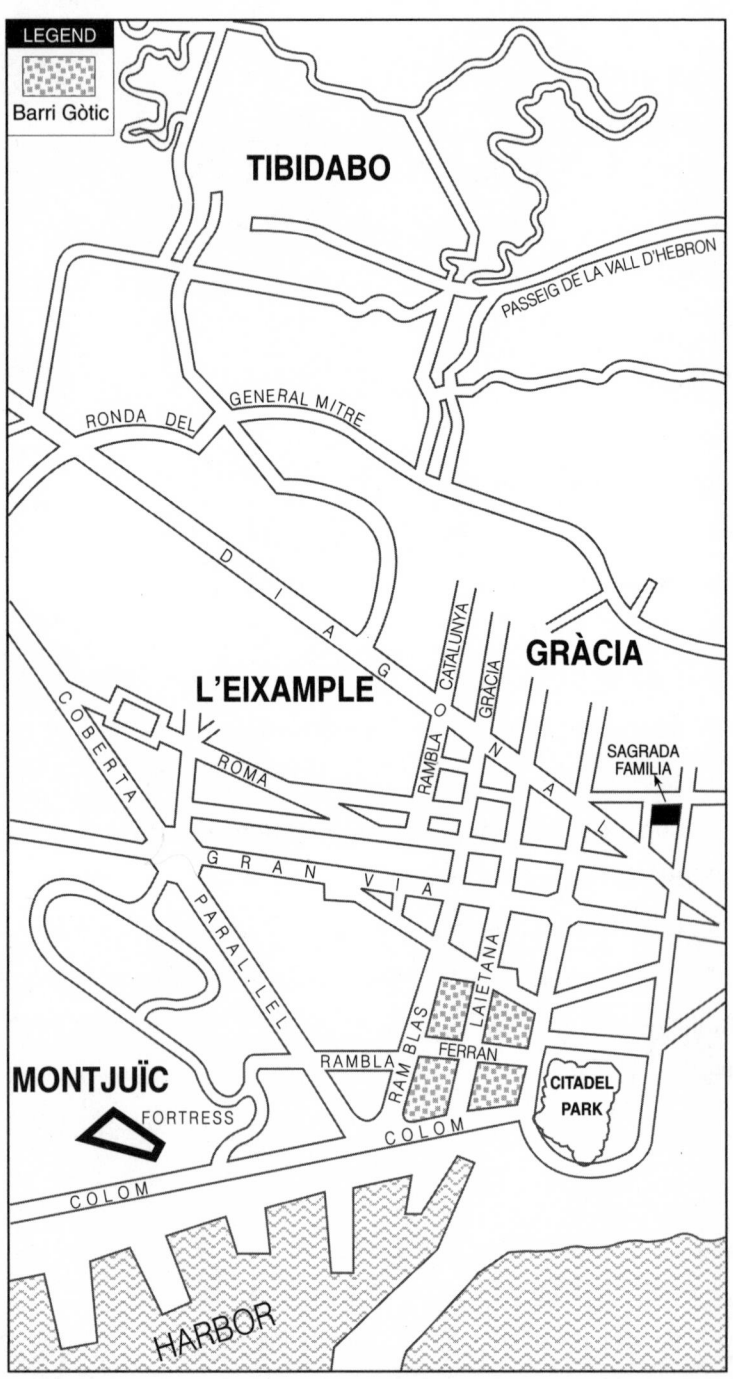

TIBIDABO

PASSEIG DE LA VALL D'HEBRON

GENERAL MITRE

RONDA DEL

DIAGONAL

L'EIXAMPLE

GRÀCIA

CATALUNYA

GRACIA

RAMBLA

VIA ROMA

COBERTA

GRAN VIA

SAGRADA FAMILIA

PARAL·LEL

LAIETANA

RAM BLAS

RAMBLA

FERRAN

MONTJUÏC

FORTRESS

CITADEL PARK

COLOM

COLOM

HARBOR

INTRODUCTION
Glitz and Grit

"The definitive Barcelona novel doesn't exist, and never will. If such a novel were to appear one day, it would mean that our city would have ripped off its masks, revealed all its secrets, rejected all inventiveness. Our words would become void of spirit."

—Montserrat Roig, novelist and essayist

Barcelona author Manuel Vásquez Montalbán refers to the "various distinct Barcelonas that coexist" and the "different buried cities." To the first-time visitor, Barcelona's charms seem obvious, almost blatant: one of the world's great promenades, *Las Ramblas*; the playful and astonishing architectural wonders of Gaudí and the modernists; the methodical *sardana* folkdance and its organic solidarity; the playful primary colors of Miró; the rejuvenating power of the medieval Gothic Quarter; the very European cafe-

Typical dark street scene from the Gothic Quarter.

bar culture; clothing hanging to dry from centuries-old balconies in La Barceloneta; a sweet language that became an intrinsic expression of courage and resistance; and, for a perfect picture, the sea.

Beneath this surface is a whole world of ancient codes, secret passageways, and gritty back streets. To write about Barcelona is a humbling process. You must pay homage to the dazzling things that everyone sees, for they form a design that is unlike any other urban setting in the world. The city of Barcelona knows it is beautiful, for during the night it directs bright lighting upon its many gothic and modernist landmarks, and its designer cafes proudly announce the names of their architects.

Beyond these brilliant night shapes and patterns are dark inner corridors and marginalized outer neighborhoods where few visitors bother to stray. A neighborhood cafe where protesters are planning their next demonstration against the global economy. A conference room where a foreign entrepreneur is receiving free consultation on a major business project. A "social center" in an abandoned building taken over by young squatters who vie for the title of most elaborately pierced body. An apartment gathering where football heretics secretly root *against* the beloved Barça football team. A gallery in the chic Gothic Quarter rented by a collective of struggling artists, both locals and foreigners, who are now beginning to make an impact in the art world. A talented jazz saxophonist improvising his search for a market. Proletarian opera lovers. Reserved traditionalists who shed their inhibitions on the beach. People once under siege who emerged with the intact belief that you're a good guy until you prove otherwise. Secret sauces that seem to express, through the palate, an inherent human warmth and a latent exhibitionism. The shameless cultivation of a "we're number one" business psychology. Down-and-outers conjuring up creative survival strategies. And the dramatic, multiple-nuance struggle to preserve a centuries-old local language in the age of the global culture, which unfolds without respite on various fronts: between parents and their children, storekeepers and their customers, entrepreneurs and employees, natives and immigrants, natives and other natives, Barcelona and Madrid.

On its surface, Barcelona is so stunning and appealing that many visitors see no need to go any deeper. This book pays homage to the dazzling facades and then ventures inward.

Chapter One

SETTING
Identity and Public Space

"The new voices of technology have tended recently to say that the traditional city is going to find itself replaced by a series of telemetric networks, which will constitute a city without a site. This is anthropological and ecological nonsense which stems from certain political ideas. It is a vision put forward by those opposed to the collective and in favour of the privatization of the public domain."

—From a speech by architect Oriol Bohigas,
a key player in the rejuvenation of Barcelona,
at the ceremony in which the city of Barcelona received
the Gold Medal of the Royal Institute of British Architects

The objective of this book is to make it as easy as possible for the newcomer to adapt to and become enriched by Barcelona. An awareness of this city's extraordinary history is a prerequisite for fitting in. But what history are we talking about? A chronological history with a series of events, marriages of royal families, plagues, economic booms and busts, periodic bellicose conflicts with few winners and many losers, and a series of patriotic dates? Such a history can be earnestly read and then forgotten as soon as the information loses its usefulness.

We must search for the essence of this history, the dominant and memorable themes that make their impact felt in contemporary times.

After having lived in this idiosyncratic city and read enough background material for an advanced degree, three particular themes rise to the surface as Barcelona's living history, themes that must be considered in order to relate to the city's current reality. They are:

Barcelona versus Madrid: for centuries, Barcelona's primary rival has been its own central government. Spain's periodic assaults and repressive measures against Catalunya have achieved the opposite of their intended effect; the fact that the Catalans have felt their culture was under siege has made them more tenacious in defending their cultural identity, and especially their beloved language. Even after post-Franco autonomy, Catalonia still remembers. The irony: an essentially conservative need to maintain traditional culture inspired Catalonia's independent direction, yet it was the most conservative Spanish governments that most repressed Catalan autonomy. Socialists in Catalonia are less likely to be cultural nationalists, yet socialists in Madrid have been more likely to respect Catalan autonomy.

Municipal dilemmas: Surrounded by a rampart that failed to keep out invaders but that kept the local population compressed into a hyper-dense agglomeration, what happened when the walls came down and the city expanded? Today's Barcelona is the result of both visionary city planning and hopeless anarchistic development. The quality of life of the neighborhood you choose as a home will be directly linked to the extraordinary history of city planning, unbridled speculation or playful architects. Central to the tug-of-war between speculators and planners was the struggle to protect and nurture public space.

Barcelona and the world: as a port, Barcelona has enjoyed great advantages in trading with the rest of the world. When it came to world trade fairs and other international events, the city became an ad hoc capital of Spain. Barcelona's contemporary business savvy is part cause and part result of this unique history. As Barcelona leads Spain into the global, electronic culture, a broad sector of its population is entrenched in defending local diversity and a community-centered logic based on human contact.

Geographers will note that all three of these grand historical themes have much to do with Barcelona's physical setting at the outer, northern edge of Spain, compressed between mountains and sea, with a natural portal to the rest of the world.

Barcelona versus Madrid

I was about to become a witness to a musical miracle. The great Catalan jazz pianist, Tete Monteliu, was playing a special concert, accompanied by a band from the Barcelona music school, at the "casino" a few blocks from our apartment. I got there early and then watched as the blind pianist was escorted to the stage.

The Portuguese bandleader lifted his arm and counted in Spanish, "uno, dos, tres, cuatro…"

Suddenly, the people in the audience whistled their disapproval. I had no idea why, until the bandleader stopped, and began the count again, "una, dues, tres, quatre…" in Catalan!

My wife and I had been purchasing fresh chicken, sardines and wine at a local grocery, where the woman who owned the store had gladly spoken Spanish with us, or what they called *Castellano*. They knew we were from abroad. But as the summer arrived and tourists from Madrid and other parts of Spain straggled in, we noticed that when the visitors spoke Spanish to her, she would answer them defiantly in Catalan.

13

The story of Catalonia's resentment against Madrid goes back centuries. Like Spanish, Catalan is a romance language, reflecting the fact that the Romans were the first recorded settlers in the region, dating back to 218 BC. Tarragona was Rome's main outpost in the region, but today's Gothic Quarter of Barcelona was built upon the Roman settlement of *Barcino*.

In the fourth century, Franc invaders broke through the Roman ramparts of Barcino, to be followed by the Romanized Visigoths in 415. In 711, it was the Muslims' turn. Fighting their way up from Gibraltar, the Moors had little trouble defeating the Visigoths, who had been self-destructing by warring amongst themselves. The Moors would remain in much of Spain until 1492, but in 805, King Louis le Pieux, son of Charlemagne, established a Carolingian administration that included Catalonia. Neither Castillian nor Catalan was yet an established language at the time. The term "Catalan" as a language was first mentioned in documents as of the tenth century, when what is today known as the Catalan language resembled the *langue d'oc* spoken on the French side of the Pyrenees.

Political power in the Catalan region, on both sides of the Pyrenees, was in the hands of a clan of counts, led by Guifré el Pelós (hairy), who entered Barcelona in 878 and established religious organizations throughout Catalonia. Guifré was responsible for consolidating the first Catalan power structure. In the tenth century, the House of Barcelona was one of the only isolated Christian states within the Moorish Iberian Peninsula. The Moors under Al'Mansur returned in 985. The Catalan counts asked for French help to repel the Moors but the Carolingians never came to the rescue.

Only a medieval specialist can sort out the complex alliances of the time between Muslim and Christian kings during the Catholic "Reconquest" of the peninsula. The Catalan Count Ramon Berenguer, with Moorish financial support, was able to extend the Christian Catalan empire into southern France. While under Ramon Berenguer III, for the half century at the end of the 1000s and the beginning of the 1100s, Catalonia became a maritime power. This Christianization of Catalonia occurred long before the Catholic kings established total control of what would become Spain in 1492.

From the 1100s through the beginning of the 1200s, Catalonia's royalty came under the influence of neighboring Aragon. Catalonia eventually lost its territory on the French side of the Pyrenees but expanded eastward to the Islas Baleares and as far as Sardinia and Naples. Barcelona now dominated commerce with Africa and the Middle East, and Catalan-Aragon imperialism was responsible for bloody wars throughout the Mediterranean.

Within the 1200s, still before the advent of a Spanish nation, Catalonia had already established its own legal foundations as a state. In 1274, the *Consell dels Cents Jurats* became an electoral body that appointed municipal leaders, and in 1283, *les Corts Catalanes* met for the first time as a type of power base for the local merchant class against an emerging royal elite that would eventually coalesce around a nation called Spain. Although merchants financed the Catalan state, politically and socially they were considered a notch below in class by the local royalty, the Counts. The permanent government of the Corts Catalanes was referred to as *La Generalitat*, a name and an institution that has periodically evolved, been disbanded, but ultimately survived to the present day. *La Generalitat* is the name of today's Catalonia government.

By the 1400s, a combination of circumstances led to the decline of the Catalan empire: the rise of the Ottomans, resistance from colonized places like Sardinia, a devastating bubonic plague in Barcelona, and the death of the last descendant of the counts, who left no inheritor. These events coincided with the rise of the Catholic kings, who would absorb Catalonia into the Spanish state.

Barcelona's economic independence persisted with the help

15

of a community of converted Jews. At this point in history, Spain began to put the squeeze on Catalonia. The Inquisition decimated this "New Christian" sector of Barcelona's Jewish population, the Catholic kings prohibited direct trade between Catalonia and the Spanish colonies, and the Crown stiffened Catalonia's tax obligations. Catalonia was relegated to the status of any one of Spain's overseas possessions.

Castillian oppression sparked a response. In the seventeenth century, the Catalans rebelled, declared their independence, and looked to France for protection. The typical royal family intrigues eventually left Catalonia unprotected, with centralist King Felipe V threatening to once and for all eliminate the Republic of Catalonia. Between 1713 and 1714, Barcelona resisted the incursions of the Spanish Crown, finally falling on September 11, 1714.

1714. This is a date to remember. The Spanish Crown abolished the Generalitat and for the first time prohibited the teaching and writing of the Catalan language. But the Catalans seized this date as a symbol of their resolve. By attempting to crush Catalonia, the Crown became a primary catalyst of Catalan nationalism and identity, which would resurface under different guises through the next two centuries.

As Barcelona industrialized at the end of the nineteenth century, a strong anarchist-led labor movement engaged in frequent clashes with the Spanish central government. The Corts Catalanes were reestablished, and a new literature emerged when the Catalan language was once more widely spoken.

This was happening within the larger context of the "Generation of '98", a group of Spanish writers who, reacting to the defeat of Spain in the Spanish-American War, developed an internal critical view of culture that questioned many Spanish traditions.

Defeated troops from the Spanish-American War arrived at the port of Barcelona, only to find the city's merchant class decimated by the loss of Spain's last overseas colonies. What they witnessed on the streets of Barcelona was not so different from the wars they'd come from. A pedestrian would walk down one street and encounter gangs of organized thugs. Turning in the other direction, the same pedestrian would come upon bands of rebellious anarchists. Such street-life was hardly conducive to tourism. The debilitated merchant class turned to the thugs for defense against the anarchists, and eventually many of the thugs donned suits and ties and became masters of the new economy, replacing the people who had hired them. (See Eduardo Mendoza's *La Ciudad de los Prodigios*)

1909. The *Setmana Trágica*. Madrid attempted to draft young Catalan men to serve in North African wars, and the workers responded by burning churches and rioting. Anarchists were rounded up by the unpopular Spanish Civil Guards and many workers were executed. Some citizens saw the anarchists as "the enemy of their enemy", and as a result, the CNT (the anarchist *Confederación Nacional de Trabajo*) developed a powerful influence in the city's political landscape.

1923. Once again, Madrid intervened. A coup placed dictator Miguel Primo de Rivera in control of Spain. He took strong measures to repress all manifestations of Catalan culture, prohibiting both the CNT and merchant political organizations, and even shutting down Barcelona's Barça soccer club. (Today, when the Real Madrid soccer team comes into town, historical nostalgia surfaces and many Catalans see it as Barça versus Primo de Rivera.)

When Primo de Rivera was overthrown in 1930, Catalonia declared its autonomy, under the leadership of socialist Lluís Companys, and the Generalitat was again reconstituted. The anarchists took things a few steps further, occupying factories and businesses, and establishing an egalitarian way of life. Reluctant noblemen stashed their rococo clothing under the bed and went out into the street in overalls. In reaction to the 1936 coup by Franco's fascists, Barcelona's CNT took control of the city, creating its own version of the 1871 Paris Commune.

The struggle against Franco became fragmented when anarchist and Trotskyite militias seeking land reform and workers' control were undermined by the Stalinist communist party. The Stalinists, under orders from the Soviet Union, sustained an ideology of postponing the revolution in order to first defeat the fascists. Western Europe maintained a hands-off approach even though Franco's phalangists were benefiting from considerable support from Italian and German fascists. The legitimately elected Spanish Republic received aid only from the Soviet Union and Mexico's revolutionary president Lázaro Cárdenas.

For a brief period, Barcelona had the feel of a socialist republic, but without the centralized party autocracy so characteristic of failed twentieth century socialist experiments. President Companys watched history evolve beyond his control. Independent socialists from around the world descended upon Barcelona, in search of a potential utopia, among them George Orwell. (See George Orwell's *Homage to Catalonia*)

Barcelona became the focal point of resistance against the fascists. There were times, however, when Russian-supported communists within Catalonia seemed more bent on putting down the anarchists than in uniting to defeat the fascists. In a setting of internal discord, the antifascist forces fell to Franco in January of 1939.

With Franco in power and Madrid in control, it was 1714 all over again. The Generalitat was yet again abolished and the Catalan language suppressed. Spanish was named "the official language", and all public signs and even names of cities were Hispanicized. Tens of thousands of Republicans were executed. The exiled Companys was captured by the Gestapo in France and returned to Spain. At his execution, Companys shouted "Long live Catalonia".

18

The Catalans were not about to take Madrid's brutally violent no for an answer and resisted in a variety of ways, usually in secrecy. When citizens dared use the Catalan language in public, the sound of Catalan acquired the tone of epic poetry. The anarchists resisted the Franco dictatorship, first with bombings and when that didn't work, with methods of creative nonviolence.

In Mexico, President Cárdenas received the Catalan patriot Josep Tarradellas as head of Catalonia's "parliament in exile".

One musician interviewed by this reporter used his concerts to fan the embers of *catalanisme*. At public concerts in Barcelona's Gothic Palau de la Música, choirs would disobey the rules by singing in Catalan. Michener quotes a witness to such a concert:

"Did you happen to attend that great performance of Haydn's *The Seasons* at the Palau de la Música? Notice how the soloists imported from England and Germany sang in German. But the choir, God bless it, sang only in Catalan."

Michener also passes on the anecdote of the Madrileño editor of *La Vanguardia* (Barcelona's most influential newspaper) who discovered a parish priest delivering a sermon in Catalan. The editor reported the priest to the police. A parishioner heard what had happened and spread the word, and overnight, "almost every major business had canceled its advertising in *Vanguardia*." The people had masked their true sense of protest by declaring: "How can we advertise with a man who abuses a priest?" The editor was replaced. (See James Michener's *Iberia: Spanish Travels and Reflections*, "Barcelona", pp. 540–621)

Following the 1973 death of Franco, Tarradellas returned, and the Generalitat was reestablished. Catalan nationalist Jordi Pujol, reelected again and again since 1980 when he replaced Tarradellas as president of the Generalitat, will eventually break Franco's record for political longevity.

Other linguistically different parts of Spain, such as Galicia and the Basque Country, were to benefit, along with Catalonia, from the Spanish socialist government's new laws on regional autonomy, but each region has had its own interpretation. In the Basque Country, a guerrilla movement's senseless bombings isolate it from Basque nationalists.

Catalonia has created a more mellow solution. Remembering the devastating effects of internal strife during the resistance against the assault of the fascists, Catalans have resolved potential contradictions by voting for a schizophrenic equilibrium between the conservative Pujol in the Generalitat and the socialist Maragall and his cohorts at City Hall. In 1999, Maragall and Pujol squared off in an electoral race for president of the Generalitat. In a tight election, Maragall beat Pujol by a small margin, but neither had more than half the popular vote. Following electoral alliances with smaller parties, the perennial Pujol was able to remain in bloom. As usual, Pujol got more votes in smaller traditionalist cities and rural Catalonia while Maragall outscored Pujol in Barcelona.

The repeated attempts to abolish the Generalitat and prohibit the Catalan language have left the Catalans with a tenacious will to defend their culture. Catalanism has many nuances and the visitor should expect to find an entire spectrum of social thinking on the subject. Whether they want to or not, newcomers setting up stakes in Barcelona will become part of the ongoing polemic. Will immigration weaken the Catalan language? If so, how can immigrants be enticed to learn Catalan? Most Barcelonans are not heavy-handed about forcing Catalan on newcomers, and the immigrant will feel little pressure to learn the language. But the issue never disappears from the Op Ed pages of *La Vanguardia* and other media. (See "The Joys of Catalan" section in the next chapter)

Today most Catalans are content to see their language used in government and schools, to applaud the autonomy of their Generalitat, and to root for their beloved Barça to defeat Real

Madrid. But occasionally a defiant poster or graffiti can be observed, with a message like *Aco no és espanya* (This is not Spain).

Municipal Dilemmas: a Chronological Stroll

In the mid-1800s, the city fathers of Paris were heard to lament about their urban population density. Across the channel, in the late 1850s, London had only 86 inhabitants per hectare, while Paris had 356. Madrid was also confronting a population density problem, with 384 inhabitants per hectare.

During that time, wealthy Barcelona inhabitants would travel to Paris in order to experience elbowroom. Barcelona's 1860 population density was 859 inhabitants per hectare! While it is true that mountains to the west and the sea to the east constrict the growth of Barcelona, at that time there was ample undeveloped flatlands and foothill country outside the clogged city. Barcelona residents were confronted with a psychic barrier, the surrounding ancient rampart that had never served as protection against invading religious hordes, pillagers and conquerors, but had paralyzed the city's inhabitants from moving beyond the wall.

As of 1753, people were no longer confined to the old city and its central Gothic Quarter, as a new neighborhood was inaugurated, with the type of straight streets rarely seen in Spain or its colonies, even though they were mandated by colonial city planners. This was La Barceloneta, once with its back to the sea, today the city's second historical neighborhood that protects its old village atmosphere in spite of its renovated sea front.

The nineteenth century city's unbelievable density is an easy target for caricatures by Barcelona chroniclers. Eduardo Mendoza writes that "such cramped quarters were an attack against hygiene: the slightest illness was transformed into an epidemic".

The simplest solution would have been to knock down the rampart. But once more the contradiction between Madrid and Barcelona was to have a negative impact on Barcelona residents.

21

For defensive as well as strategic reasons, the government in Madrid refused permission for the walls to come down.

No one residing within the ramparts had their own private living space. It really got tight when six people lived together in a 6 m by 6 m room. The caricature of one chronicler illustrates the lack of privacy: "Rare is the Barcelona resident who has not received an imagistic account of the circumstances in which he was conceived."

The newcomer to Barcelona can get a visual sense of the city's history with a chronological walking tour. A linear stroll through the city would be fitting for William Faulkner or James Joyce, jumping ahead in time, then passing through flashbacks, only to step across an imaginary line into the future.

This is the easy option for the stroller: forget the plot and just walk in straight lines. The more challenging option is the chronological walk, which will require many more kilometers, but whose imagery will march with the city's history.

Gothic Quarter

For author Manuel Vásquez Montalbán, many of the distinct but coexisting Barcelonas are buried from the casual observer's vision, and must be deciphered. His tangible metaphor for this hidden nature of the city is the ancient Roman city where we can begin our walk, by descending into the Museu d'Historia de la Ciutat and seeing what is left of this early Barcelona. Our historical walk continues in the medieval Gothic Quarter (Barri Gòtic), with its asymmetrical maze of narrow and winding streets and alleys. Begin at the Plaça Sant Jaume, surrounded by the Palau de la Generalitat and the Ajuntament, the Catalunya and municipal government buildings respectively, where the conservatives in the Generalitat and the socialists in the Ajuntament have nurtured a peaceful and civil balance of powers.

The main plaza offers a semblance of elbowroom before entering the cramped medieval labyrinth above the Roman city.

Another plaza-size illusion of leaving the labyrinth is found at the plaza facing the Gothic Cathedral. Many of the other alleyways masquerading as streets are too narrow for automobile traffic; what you lose in space you gain in tranquility.

Author Santiago Rusinol once suggested that such streets be used for the frequent anarchist demonstrations, so that one would easily count how many demonstrators passed by.

Part of the fun of the Barri Gòtic is getting lost there. One stumbles upon quirky restaurants, noisy bars, intimate plazas, upscale boutiques with rustic stonewall interiors, or massive peeling wood doors at gritty dead ends, always in the shadows of ornate facades and sculpted window frames.

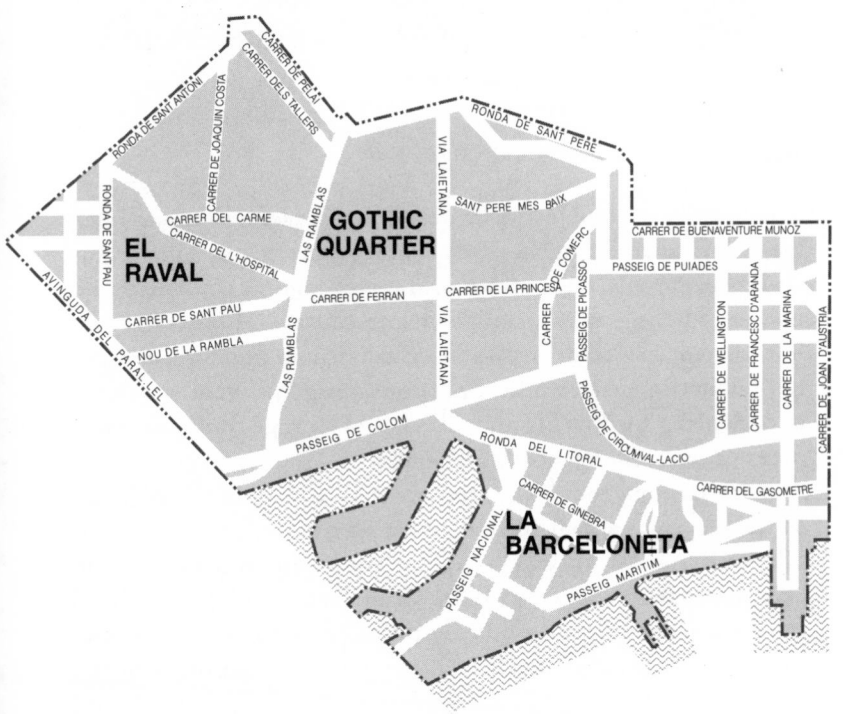

For some people the Ramblas is where it's happening. For others this is a way to cross from the Gothic Quarter to El Raval.

El Raval

After you've soaked in the medieval ambiance, it's time to relive the habits of many of the 19th century Barri Gòtic inhabitants. Cross La Rambla, one of the world's most famous boulevards and public gathering places, and delve into El Raval. El Raval, meaning "outside the wall" in Arabic, was once an impoverished and uninhibited quarter where Barcelona residents went slumming, experiencing the low life and all types of strange trades, of which prostitution was the most traditional.

Separating the old quarter from El Raval, La Rambla acts as the old city's spinal cord, connecting different historical periods with a long and wide strolling area, with automobile lanes on either side. You get the ornate Gran Teatre del Liceu, the traditional market, Mercat de la Boqueria, and other vintage sites, but you also get McDonald's, a wax museum and other blatant reminders of the invasion of tourist and global culture. Divided into different sections, each with a distinct personality, from the seediest to the stateliest, one can refer to Las Ramblas in the plural.

La Barceloneta

Until now, the historical wanderer has not had to make any great sacrifices in added walking distance. But from here on in, the trajectory becomes less practical. From the southernmost tip of Las Ramblas at the Monument of Colom, one can walk north by northeast along Passeig de Colom, parallel to the seaport, to La Barceloneta. Here, the straight and narrow streets lined with cramped colonial apartment buildings, clothing drying on balconies, and a salty sea breeze remind some travelers of parallel scenes in Old Havana. La Barceloneta is the gateway to the Olympic Village, but it would be the sacrilegious equivalent of time travel for the historical stroller to jump from the 1753 Barceloneta to the 1992 Olympic Village.

The sun rarely enters the narrow streets of La Barceloneta, with its collages of drying clothing.

25

L'Eixample

After a seafood lunch in La Barceloneta, within the dark corridors of the village proper or on the sea front outside, the stroll crosses back through the Ciutat Vella (Old City) that contains the Barri Gòtic, or to avoid the flashback, hop on a metro from La Barceloneta to Plaça Catalunya. Then walk north into l'Eixample (the Extension), city planner Ildefons Cerdá's 1867 "integral village". For the most part the streets are straight, with a diagonal boulevard aptly named La Diagonal facilitating through traffic. Street corners are clipped away so that crosswalks are a few meters inside from the corner itself, creating octagonal blocks.

Once l'Eixample had become an established community, art nouveau buildings by Gaudi and his modernist cohorts began to spice up the neighborhood.

Barcelona's most amazing landmark, Gaudi's unfinished neo-Gothic La Sagrada Familia, is found within the northeast sector of l'Eixample. On a shortlist of the most impressive modern city landmarks, based on pure aesthetics, La Sagrada Familia would have to be given preference over the Eiffel Tower, the Statue of Liberty, or the Washington Monument. An important cluster of gingerbread Gaudi building-sculptures can be appreciated along Passeig de Gràcia, directly north of Plaça de Catalunya, in the direction of Plaça de Joan Carlos I.

26

What modernist architects added to the l'Eixample sector at the turn of the century partially compensates for what was taken away. The visionary Cerdá laid out a grid that included numerous green areas, as public plazas and inner patios of multifamily dwellings. Many of these green areas were enveloped by the rabid property speculation that followed the inauguration of l'Eixample. Purchasers of real estate divided their property in two and sold the second half for a profit. The new purchasers followed suit, but this time they were dividing half a tract into two smaller pieces. It was a type of pyramid scheme, with the later purchasers buying the smallest lots or houses for the highest prices.

Construction workers get to know Gaudí's La Sagrada Familia better than we do.

Ajuntament de Barcelona

Gaudí's Casa Batlló from two perspectives.

29

La Ciutadella

From the southeasternmost corner of l'Eixample, it's a short walk to the next step in the city's architectural and social history: Parc de la Ciutadella. The fortress, referred to as La Ciutadella, was Madrid's foothold in Catalunya, demolished in 1869. This quarter, as you see it today, is rooted in the year 1888, when it was assigned to host Barcelona's World Exposition, criticized at the time as being a white elephant. In a city not known for its abundance of green areas, the Ciutadella Park offers welcome relief for the harassed urbanite. The gateway to this sector, a red-bricked Arabesque style Arc de Triomf, is a more colorful designed version of its Paris and Washington Square counterparts.

Also built for the World Expo was a modernist stone sculpture with a waterfall leading into a pleasant lake. The Gaudiesque designs that decorate the falls were built in the years prior to the Expo, suggesting that Gaudi had his precursors, or that perhaps he had a hand in the project. On a hot summer day, the shady city zoo offers refreshing relief for the urban trekker.

Gràcia

Once more it's time for the historical wanderer to avoid a flashback by taking a short metro ride to Gràcia, to the immediate north of l'Eixample. Chronological purists encounter their first contradiction in this neighborhood. Its narrow streets and intimate plazas situate it in pre-l'Eixample, even pre-La Barceloneta, but its avantgarde literary cafes and intimate plazas clearly set it in the twentieth centuries. Its working class, revolutionary history belongs to both the nineteenth and twentieth century. But chronological purists will note that it was incorporated into the city of Barcelona in the last decade of the nineteenth century. Within a brisk walk from the tourist core of the city and with unbeatable old-neighborhood charm, Gràcia's daily life has somehow remained insulated from commercial tourism, as most foreign visitors to Barcelona tend to remain within the invisible rampart.

Daniel Giordano Leis

You never know what street festival you'll encounter in Gràcia, a great neighborhood.

31

Manuel Iglesias

Scene from Parc Guëll.

Parc Guëll

Our preliminary, imaginative historical walking tour now hops north and crosses the Travessera de Dalt for hardly more than a kilometer from the northern edge of Gràcia for the next addition to Barcelona. Walking is one of the world's healthy pleasures. People who do not walk as much as they'd like to, for lack of aesthetic interest in the surroundings, should consider moving here. Barcelona is no treadmill, and many a nook and cranny offers surprising nuances of imaginative charm. Perhaps the most surreal of all Barcelona walking experiences is found within the Parc Guëll, the next stop on our introductory tour.

Imagine yourself as an aspiring artist with an unlimited supply of bricks, mosaic tiles, cement, and stones. You are given free rein in a huge park and told by your benefactor that you will be allowed to make exciting and colorful roads lined with sprawling and twisting arched stone walls leading to buildings sculpted with a dazzling array of materials and colors, and that you'll be paid for it. You have your choice of Roman, Gothic, Moorish, and any fanciful modernist combinations of these styles, and you can abide by the expensive Gaudi principle that straight lines must be prohibited since they do not exist in nature. This was the happy fate of Antoni Gaudi in 1900, when Count Eusebi Guëll decided to create a "Disneyland" in his hilly property to the north of the city. As a business, the project failed because of an overabundance of aesthetics and a lack of commercial attractions, but what was completed became a miracle of landscape art.

El Barrio Chino

Around the time when Parc Guëll was being designated a public garden in 1922, the mythology of Barcelona in Europe was being forged by a neighborhood called Chinatown (Barrio Chino). The Chinese quarter had little or nothing to do with Barcelona's few Chinese residents. Between the 1920s and '30s, the Barrio Chino was known for its erotic and seedy splendor.

Its site is on and around the southernmost part of Las Ramblas, ending at the port, extending west to Avinguda del Paral.lel and to the east to the medieval quarter. Prostitutes, ruffians, billiard hustlers, beggars, street musicians, sailors, and immigrants gave this neighborhood its emblems. George Orwell stayed here when on leave from the war front. A decade ago, the Barrio Chino had become a caricature of itself, inhabited by a "less picturesque, sadder, and uselessly aggressive underpopulation," according to Vásquez Montalbán, more similar to the Pigalle district of Paris or the pre-gentrified 42nd Street in New York. Today, it's been gentrified, and a discreet plaza with X-rated peep shows is about all that's left of the original Barrio Chino.

Montjuïc

Directly east-southeast from the edge of the Barrio Chino is the next visual epoch of Barcelona: the wooded hill of Montjuïc (Jewish hill). Here we are obligated to make several flashbacks and fast forwards. These were the high periods of Barcelona's Jewish community or when Montjuïc's fruit orchards offered a country escape from the claustrophobic Ciutat Vella. The Montjuïc castle served as military quarters from which the forces from Madrid could send bombs thundering down upon the city during the 1840s rebellions, the same castle that later became a prison. Fast forward to the present day when the castle has become a military museum and we find Olympic facilities including a historic soccer stadium, the Joan Miró Foundation, an avant-garde structure featuring the work of one of Catalonia's great artists, and a breathtaking teleferic taking non-climbers to the upper portions of this polyfunctional park.

But Montjuïc's greatest historic claim to fame was as a site of Barcelona's second World Exposition in 1929. Not only does the stadium extend back to that date, but also to what Michener calls the world's first theme park: Poble Espanyol, with eighty-one buildings whose exteriors faithfully copied original structures

34

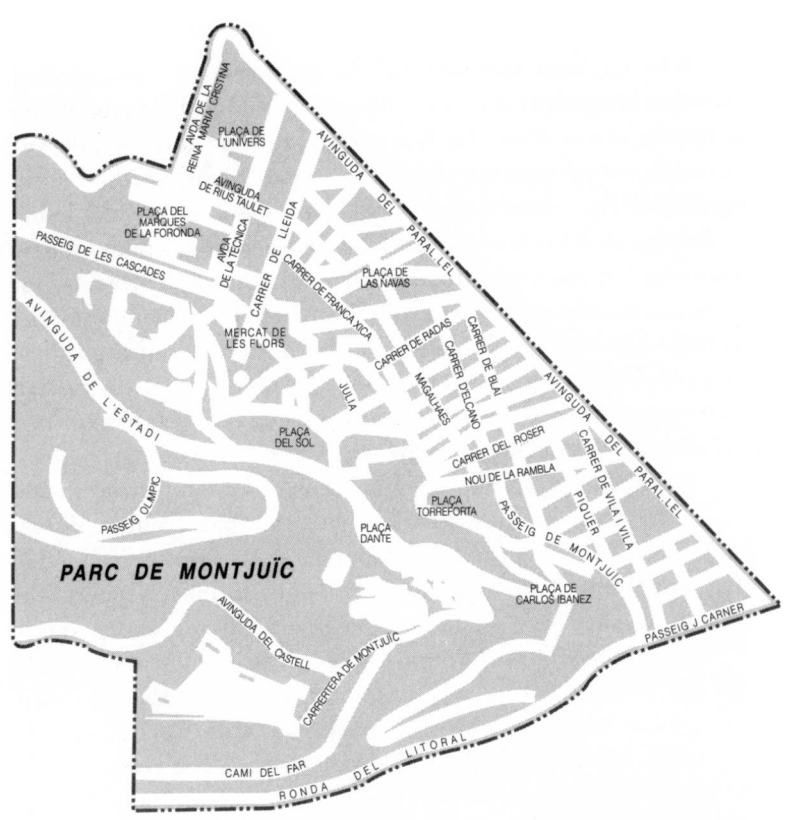

and streets from throughout Spain, stone by stone, "a synthesis of all that is most typical in Spain" according to the author-traveler. For months while living in Barcelona we refused to visit Poble Espanyol, assuming it was just another tourist trap. Luckily we succumbed to our curiosity, going there to find regional artisans, a cleverly concocted ambiance that somehow acquired a life of its own, and spirited nightlife.

My opinion: Poble Espanyol is not your typical theme park.

My critics': that my liking this place disqualifies me from my identification as an iconoclast.

See and judge for yourself.

35

Like the 1888 World Expo, the 1929 version was criticized as a waste of scarce resources and money, a whim of dictator Primo de Rivera. As in 1888, Madrid wanted to have the fair but was not forthcoming with all the funds to pay for it, and the municipality of Barcelona suffered the consequences. But the living landmarks that have remained from these expos demand a new evaluation of the cost-effectiveness of such great projects, for certain structures have remained sustainable throughout the century. A less tangible benefit is that both expos saved large green areas of the city from the rampant speculation that dominated other sectors, during a period of history when concepts like ecology and green areas belonged to the realm of science fiction.

Until the 1992 Villa Olimpica replaced an industrial wasteland and gypsy squatters' terrain just up the coast from La Barceloneta, much of the urban development of Barcelona declined in character. Functional high-rise apartment buildings typical of the Franco era have little aesthetic appeal (with notable exceptions in the work of the architect Antoni Tàpies). Vásquez Montalbán calls this the "destructive will of Francoism", and writes that the "local bourgeoisie" was "partially responsible for the destruction of artistic, urban patrimony built by their ancestors". The consequence: buildings without much personality, narrow sidewalks placing streets under the dominion of the all-powerful automobile, and the disappearance of public gathering places, which fit within the objectives of fascism of suppressing freedom of expression.

But according to Vásquez Montalbán himself, once democracy was reestablished in the 1970s, Barcelona made an inventory of its urban wounds. Democracy has renovated many of its bars and plazas, the gathering places of public discourse, although at some of these, the music is too loud for an exchange of ideas. Beyond the limits of the 1930s city, however, "uniformized neighborhoods ... engage in open combat on an uneven playing field against the international cultural banalizers." Such assaults have hit Barcelona in its most historical neighborhoods, with "McDonald's and other companies which, not content with rallying all the uncultivated and avidly youthful stomachs, has transformed noble buildings in beautiful neighborhoods into supermarkets with bovine tumors with transfusions of ketchup..."

(With all due respect for Europeans like Vásquez Montalbán who use McDonald's as a whipping boy, the international burger corporation does serve three important social functions:

- *Emergency toilets.* International travelers unaware of how to find emergency bathrooms in public libraries and government buildings have been overheard to exclaim, "God bless the Golden Arches."
- *Cost-of-living statistics.* Travelers in need of comparing the cost of living between different European countries can simply use the cost of a Big Mac as a yardstick.
- *Fussy children.* Parents can find refuge for their small children when a thunderstorm moves in.)

This post-expo Barcelona described by Vásquez Montalbán, built between the 1940s and '60s, mainly in periphery neighborhoods, is worth a visit. The walks are long and aesthetic moments few and far between. But, hidden behind the apparent alienation is a subversive wave of cultural resistance. Old world bakers, shoemakers, bartenders, adult education specialists, and even community organizers still provide homespun personal service from their cubbies set into the first floors of block-long high rises.

Pedralbes

On the next-to-last leg of our introductory walking tour, we visit the southwest inner suburb of Pedralbes, where Eduardo Mendoza's fictional extraterrestrial visitor found "the elegance of its houses, the seclusion of its streets, the luxuriance of its lawns, and crowdedness of its swimming pools." Mendoza's extraterrestrial wonders why Barcelonans now living in drab and congested highrise neighborhoods have not chosen to live in Pedralbes instead.

The most predictable excursion from Pedralbes would be to drive in a sports car to the boutiqued and malled floating sea front, which in the late 1980s began expunging the gritty maritime sub-cultural atmosphere some of us still yearn for. Result: the Maremagnum mall, discos, floating theaters, upscale pubs, a state-of-the-art aquarium, and a World Trade Center.

Olympic Village

Finally, beginning at La Barceloneta, we have a most pleasant and refreshing walk, northeast along the boardwalk of the city's renovated and attractive sea front. To the right, the sea. To the left, the Olympic Village, and then, farther up the coast, old industrial zones in a state of transition, with a few vintage factories designed by modernist architects still standing. By the time this book has been published, other Ramblas will come from these newer neighborhoods, arriving in perpendicular fashion to the boardwalk.

Issues

Barcelona's most controversial decision has been what to do with Gaudi's Sagrada Familia. Destiny did not respect the unlimited playful artistic ventures inscribed in Gaudi's happy calendar, when in 1926 a streetcar ran him down. What to do with his greatest project? Leave it as it was, unfinished, says one group of purists. Use what is left of his original plans to faithfully complete the monumental structure, say other purists. Finish it, in evolving styles, as Gaudi would have done had he been alive in the 1980s and '90s, say the advocates of finishing the project. The latter argument has a solid historical foundation. What they want to do with Gaudi's neo-Gothic structure was precisely what was done with Gothic monuments from the Middle Ages, that took decades or centuries to finish, passing under the direction of different architects, and incorporating distinct architectural periods. From the looks of things, the third option, perhaps purer historically than the aesthetically purist solutions, has been the fait accompli winner. When it is eventually completed, La Sagrada Familia will be a faithful enactment of medieval architectural history and workmanship.

Another irony is that the Sagrada Familia has become an unstated nationalist image of Barcelona, since Gaudi, unlike his activist and nationalist contemporaries Lluis Domènech i Montaner and Josep Puig i Cadalfalch, was totally apolitical and couldn't care less that his great work was funded with the purposes of expiating his city from the leftist activist sins of the past, much like the Sacre Coeur project in Paris.

Barcelona's polemical relationship with its history extends far beyond La Sagrada Familia. After the ornate nineteenth century opera house Gran Teatre del Liceu, whose innards were gutted by fire in 1994, was restored to its original design, Mr. Juan Bea Girons commented in *La Vanguardia* that "the deficiencies of making the Liceu 'the same, and in the same place' has produced defective results and many disillusioned season ticket holders … Nostalgia has been very expensive."

Our preliminary chronological stroll through Barcelona finally rests at the Centre de Cultura Contemporania de Barcelona, opened in 1994: the first cultural center in Europe dedicated exclusively to the subject of cities and urban culture as a whole, on Montalegre Street, only two twisting blocks west of Plaça Catalunya. (Info in English: http://www.cccb.org/ingles/informac.htm)

What you'll see when you walk through Barcelona is an award-winning city. In 1999, the Gold Medal of the Royal Institute of British Architects, usually given to a person, was awarded to the whole city of Barcelona. According to Barcelona architect Oriol Bohigas, the city won this award because of the prevailing urban political ideology of its three socialist mayors, that "the city is the indispensable physical domain for the modern development of a coherent commonality. It is not a place of the individual, but

39

the place of individuals who together make up a community," and Oriol Bohigas speaks eloquently against the trend of "privatization of the public domain".

Sooner or later the walker in Barcelona will sense this public consciousness, observing a street concert, bumping into a political demonstration, or sharing a bench with other citizens in an intimate plaza. Whatever walking strategy you choose, to really get to know the city, avoid the rampart phenomenon. The rampart's been gone for more than a century, but tourists in Barcelona seem to be drawn within its invisible past, and many remain walled within the area that the rampart once surrounded.

Geography and Climate

No wonder Barcelona residents often combine seafood with meat in a meal (*mar i muntanya*). Their city is bounded by both natural wonders: the glorious Mediterranean Sea to the east/south and a rough and attractive range of mountains to the west/north. From the docks, the pedestrian can look back upon the city and up into the mountains. The view at night is magnificent. And from high points like Tibidabo, we can look down upon the city, with especially brilliant clear days in the fall, winter and early spring. Binoculars will enhance the experience.

For pedestrians and cyclers alike, the weather is superb compared to colder, darker cities to the north, like Paris, or to inland Madrid, with its cold winters and burning summers. Both urban trekker and outdoor cafe denizens can use this handy chart to choose the season according to their persuasions. July, August and September can be hot and humid, while winters are mild.

AVERAGE TEMPERATURES

	C	F	
January	10	50	(the sunniest month)
February	13	56	(may go below 5C/41F, with snow in nearby mountains)

March	13	56	
April	14	57	
May	18	65	
June	21	70	
July	25	78	(temperatures can go as high as 37C/99F
August	25	78	in both July and August)
September	22	72	(frequent storms)
October	18	65	(frequent storms)
November	16	61	
December	12	54	

°Unpredictable winds from the Pyrenees can bring sudden drops in temperature.
°°For those who seek the least extremes and clearest skies, the period from late April through early June is the ideal.

Barcelona and the World

In the Middle Ages, with the Mediterranean Sea as the primary maritime trade route, Barcelona found itself in a privileged situation, which it took advantage of to become an imperialist empire. Once trade became oceanic in 1492, Barcelona's influence was destined to decline, and Madrid began to dominate Iberian power struggles. But Madrid knew Barcelona was a more ideal international city and sanctioned the Catalan metropolis as the site of world expos in 1888 and 1929. And it was Barcelona and not Madrid that hosted the 1992 Olympic Games. Barcelona's international entrepreneurial savvy, based on a legendary work ethic, is a common cliché cultivated by popular and elite culture.

"The Catalans always talk about the same thing," says an extraterrestrial visitor in Eduardo Mendoza's novel, *Sin Noticias de Gurb*. "That is to say, work."

You hear about the work ethic all the time from proud Catalans, who find international commerce as a beyond regionalist type of nationalism. And in order to maintain their economic and cultural independence, Catalan nationalists look to Europe as an alternative to Madrid.

41

What Barcelona was missing in its relationship with Madrid was compensated for by Paris: the Paris-Barcelona connection, visualized in the work of Picasso and Miró, with France as Catalonia's most prolific trading partner. On an international level, in 1997, the most recent year with available statistics, Barcelona held more international conventions, 48, than any other city, outscoring Sydney, Australia by 4 conventions.

Barcelona extends its Catalan linguistic influence as far south as Valencia and north to Roussillon in southern France, but the exclusive use of Catalan in Barcelona universities limits the numbers of foreign students. Why then is the city's most influential newspaper, *La Vanguardia*, published in Castillian rather than Catalan? Must Barcelona authors write their books in Spanish to receive international attention, or on principle should they write in Catalan, knowing they'll have a smaller audience?

One thing is for sure: Barcelona residents maintain their impact on the rest of the world with the international success of their opera singers, classical and poet-musicians like Joan Manuel Serrat, and of course, their beloved soccer team, an ideal medium for synthesizing the opposites of regional pride and worldly aplomb. But has the Barça club gone too far in importing foreign players? The city's other team, scorned by many local fans because of the historical oppression associated with its name "Español," is considered by some heretic soccer fans as the real Barcelona team since it fields a large percentage of local players.

A major plot in the contemporary drama of Barcelona involves the precarious balance between fervent regionalism and unmistakable universalism. The related subplot: Catalonia's cultural conservatism as it weirdly harmonizes with Barcelona's long history of leftist revolutionary activism. Barcelona may be one of the first great cities in the world to find a successful and dynamic balance between acting locally and thinking globally.

CHAPTER TWO

PEOPLE
The Gurb Method and Other Ways to Fit In

"Of any city in Spain, Barcelona is the easiest to adjust to. You just have to get used to the Catalans. I find them refreshing. They do what they say."

—a Dutch painter who visited Barcelona and decided to stay

The word "Catalans" first appeared in writing three centuries before Spain became a nation. In the twelfth century, Pisa sent soldiers out to fight the Moors, who were wreaking havoc on Pisa's Mediterranean commerce. But the Pisanos, errant navigators in search of the Baleares islands, landed by mistake in Blanes, on the Iberian coast north of Barcelona, and started killing people. The poem *Liber Mallorichinus* notes that the attacked people, realizing the Pisanos were after the Moors, shouted, "We are Catalans, that's what they call us."

Catalan intellectual Maria Aurelia Capmany sees the irony that "the first time in which the word Catalans appeared was because the Catalans had to identify themselves".

Capmany suggests that the Catalan identity has been forged in part by external pressures: "so often our Catalan identity has been questioned, so often we've had to define the nature of being a Catalan, that it doesn't surprise me that we know this very well. There are happy peoples who do not know what they are."

"Of course," stated another Catalan intellectual, Francesc Vicens, "we've taken a defensive position, and why not, if we feel truly persecuted."

"If it hadn't been for Franco prohibiting our language," said one of my acquaintances, "you wouldn't hear so much defining of our culture today."

After having read the whole transcript of a sensitive encounter of Catalan and Castillian intellectuals who were trying to bridge the cultural gap between their two peoples, I sensed that throughout the proceedings the Catalans had avoided being boxed into a situation in which they would be forced to define themselves. While at the same time, the Castillians had exercised the utmost caution in avoiding cultural clichés about their counterparts. The subject had been too hot to handle, and in the end, both the Catalans and the Castillians had, acting like Spaniards, preferred civility to confrontation.

STEREOTYPES

Whenever foreigners land in a new culture, they must sort out the stereotypes and decide what is to be believed and what is a distortion. All too often we allow our preconceived notions to dominate our perceptions, and rationalize the stereotypes until we believe them.

In Barcelona, we will have a good deal of help from the local population, as many Catalans purposely foster certain stereotypes about themselves. "We are hardworking and frugal," they repeat in so many ways.

At first I suspected that this was simply an expression of pride at Barcelona's economic achievements. You begin to feel there's some sort of sentiment of superiority in relation to the rest of Spain, and you also perceive that such expressions are part of a defense mechanism that had to be created as part of the resistance against the Franco dictatorship. But in further research, I came across a book of old Catalan proverbs with a considerable number of sayings from long before the Spanish Civil War that highlighted frugality and the work ethic.

When a representative of an important business support organization, Barcelona Activa, referred to his people as "Calvinists", he was expressing the epitome of this fundamental Catalan self-stereotype.

Another stereotype, one more likely to come from outside Catalonia, is that the Catalans are reserved. If you come from a northern country, you'll probably disagree but if you come from the south, you may validate the cliché, which means that such stereotypes are impressionistic. My own experience includes arguments that both support and defy the stereotype.

On the one hand, the imagery of the *sardana* dance, one of the utmost expressions of Catalan culture, seems to support the generality. Dancers move in delicate and understated nuances, and individuals are absorbed by the group. There are no soloists, no virtuosos, and no show-offs. In its collective spirit it is almost the inverse of the *flamenco*.

But visit the neighborhood tavern, one of the centers of Barcelona social life, and you will receive evidence of the opposite point of view. Visitors from other "lonely crowd" cities will be surprised at how easy it is to meet people and become part of the conversation. Reserved people are usually very tentative with strangers. In Barcelona, the outgoing stranger will find a match in his or her local counterpart. Sometimes I'm taken aback that quite personal subjects can surface in a tavern conversation. And how can it be possible, one may ask, that a culture of reserved people will approve of the custom of women bathers going topless on the beach?

You don't expect reserved people to express their sentiments through touch, but foreigners who've come here from northern countries often perceive that the Catalans are not at all shy about touching to express their humanity. Back in the States, with paranoia rampant about child abusers on the loose, the Smoley children had been told to back off from the touches of affectionate adults. Within a short time after having moved to Barcelona, the Smoleys were obligated to reeducate their three children, that here it was okay if a friend, neighbor or even stranger touched them as a sign of positive affection.

Are the Catalans Calvinists with a deep-rooted work ethic? Are they reserved? Like any other place on earth, in Barcelona the whole spectrum of human behavior exists. Whether things tilt in one direction or another depends on anecdotal impressions. Just how "valid" these stereotypes are for you may depend on whether you are from a northern or southern culture. But that's another stereotype, isn't it?

Some of the very Catalans who claimed to be Calvinists or workaholics seemed far too generous to me with their valuable time to fit my view of a utilitarian Calvinist, and others too immediately affectionate to be reserved. But those are the ones I met. Maybe the ones we don't meet fit the stereotype. The best way to avoid any misleading abstract conclusions is to deal with concrete anecdotes and to quote the opinions of the Catalans themselves.

THE GURB METHOD

In his novel *Sin Noticias de Gurb*, Barcelona author Eduardo Mendoza's extraterrestrial narrator was finding it quite difficult to adjust to the city, given his "cultural" differences. It was the neighborhood bar where this character was able more or less to fit in, and he even used the bar to receive messages from his lost companion, Gurb, and his sponsors from outer space.

In both of our living experiences in Barcelona, we had no trouble finding friends and fitting in. But the first time, without the Gurb Method, it took some time. My second stay became an experiment with the Gurb Method. During my first two or three days, I visited several neighborhood bars until I found two of them where I was made to feel comfortable. From then on, I made those two bars my regular stopoffs. I soon began to receive preferential perks, conversations developed with other regulars, and these two places became homes away from home. All this happened faster than I had projected: within a week.

The cafe-bar is one of Barcelona's and Catalonia's primary social centers. There are many other ways to get involved and fit in: community organizations, social clubs, collegial at-work relationships, and getting to know neighbors at sites of commerce and plaza benches. Becoming involved in community activities and socially responsive volunteerism is certainly a fulfilling way to accomplish goals and at the same time meet people with affinities. But the cafe-bar stands out as a social focal point.

Even short-stay tourists can benefit from this strategy. Tourism can be an alienating activity. You experience places and sights as an outsider. You try to see as many things in as short a period of time as possible. This is the quantitative approach encouraged by the tourism industry, and most tourists end up having to grasp their newfound trinkets and souvenirs as material evidence that they actually were "there". The more qualitative approach is to frequent the same establishments on a daily basis and spend a large chunk of one's time in the same neighborhood. "Doing everything" in a city can result in experiencing nothing, at least not on a human scale. With this qualitative approach you will miss some of the "must" sights, but you will find fulfillment in other more humane ways.

Mendoza's extraterrestrial not only went to the cafe-bars but also decided on one particular bar and hung out at that place. In the end, when it came time to return to his planet, he decided to betray his kingdom and remain in Barcelona.

The Gurb Method has another facet. Against all odds, Gurb and his extraterrestrial partner were able to make acquaintances because they had split up and gone places alone. Traveling in pairs or groups is fun, but it segregates you from the local population. No matter how well you all get along, it is advantageous to split up from time to time. Conversations with the locals will never get off the ground if you are always talking with your partner.

Adding my own nuances to the Gurb Method, I'd extend the cafe-bar method to commerce in general. I did an obviously unscientific survey by comparing personal commerce along Las Ramblas with the same errands in my two different neighborhoods. In the tourist core, service was friendly enough but impersonal. The proprietors or employees were so accustomed to a transitory clientele that they had lost the intrinsic interest in developing long-term relationships. On the other hand, in the neighborhoods commerce was personalized to a far greater extent, and proprietors had more time to chat with clients. In the neighborhoods it didn't take long to feel like an insider.

Barcelona facades are quite satisfying, and may leave the admiring visitor so dazzled that he or she decides to remain on the outside. Barcelona interiors, both architectural and human, are splendidly exciting. The qualitative "Gurb" strategy derived from the Mendoza novel will move the visitor beyond the facades into what Mendoza's colleague Vásquez Montalbán calls the hidden Barcelona.

CUSTOMS

Knowing and adapting to a few simple local customs will improve one's chance of fitting in. When walking into a room of people or making eye contact with acquaintances and strangers alike, a *bon día* (in Catalan) or *buenos días* (in Spanish) is appropriate. When you know the person well enough, *hola* is often used, in both languages. When parting, it's *adéu/adiós*.

When renewing contact with a friend of either sex, an embrace is called for. Otherwise, a handshake will do. In commerce, regular customers and proprietors shake hands before and after doing business.

When doing business at an office or over a counter, always say "good day" before getting down to business.

It has been written that Barcelona residents usually spend time with friends in public places rather than in their homes. But we've had the experience of exchanging dinner invitations. In such cases, the invited party should bring a gift. From our anecdotal experience, flowers make for the best gift. Judging by the abundance of florist shops in the city, flowers must be quite popular. A bottle of wine is also acceptable, but you'd better know which wines are the good ones, for throughout Spain there is an abundance of cheap wines that will not do for a dinner gift.

HE'S STILL CHOOSING THE WINE

No matter how well you study the customs, social situations that call for improvisation will inevitably arise. In any new social situation, the fundamental custom is courtesy.

THE JOYS OF CATALAN

"You're speaking Catalan to make me go crazy."
"I speak Catalan with whoever I feel like."

—dialogue from *La Rosa de Alejandría*
by Manuel Vásquez Montalbán

A long-term visitor can probably get by well enough by speaking a survival mode of *Castellano*, the word locals use for what we know as the Spanish language. When we first lived in Barcelona, I figured that, with my fluent Spanish, I'd have no need to learn Catalan. But after hearing the beauty of the Catalan language, "need" was no longer an issue. If establishing good rapport is a necessity, then it pays to learn at least a few rudimentary phrases in Catalan. But beyond all practical concerns, the language is not only intriguing but, having been banned during the Franco dictatorship, a metaphor for the resistance of a whole people against homogenizing uniformity.

Once I'd realized that the Catalan language functioned as a musical accompaniment for the Catalonia landscape, I decided to dig in and try to get a grip on it. Since Catalan is somewhere between Spanish and French, my knowledge of those two languages was a great help. (Those of us who have trouble dealing with so many unpronounced syllables in French will he happy to learn that Frenchified words in Catalan are pronounced phonetically.) I began by reading the exquisite prose of Josep Pla, dictionary in hand, and other Catalan writers. My next step was to find a basic grammar text and learn whatever structures and conjugations I was not able to glean from the texts. Once you know any romance language, the next one that comes along makes sense.

Finally, by word of mouth I was able to find people who were interested in a cafe exchange: a half-hour of English for them and then a half-hour of Catalan for me. Many folks in Barcelona would love to practice their English and would be proud to showcase their Catalan as well. I still have a long way to go, but I reached a milestone when, at a public forum, I was able to raise my hand and volunteer an opinion in Catalan. I made a great effort to use words that were not similar to Spanish, for I didn't want to allow for any chance that the bilingual speaker would understand what I had to say because of my Spanish.

My knowledge of Catalan is still what they call "passive" (listening, reading and basic social and commercial phrases), but the joy of Catalan begins with the first *Hola* or *Adéu* and never lets up.

Survey

No matter how much you fumble with the language, you'll never be embarrassed or disgraced by speaking broken Catalan. With many foreigners in Barcelona choosing to bypass this language and learn only Castillian, your interest in Catalan will be greatly appreciated by the locals no matter how many mistakes you make.

In an informal survey, I decided to take a few days and start to do all my business in Catalan. I practiced the basic phrases and set out from bank to florist to photo shop to bar to pastry shop to government office to produce market. I tallied how the people reacted to my using Catalan. Approximately forty percent, hearing my *Castellano* accent, responded in Spanish. Fifty percent responded in Catalan. A majority within this largest group lit up with joy and bent over backward to help me through the exchange. Another five percent, hearing my American accent, responded in English. And the final five percent were too busy or indifferent to take me seriously. Even in my own language I tend to make a fool of myself more than five percent of the time, so the results of this survey were personally satisfying. At least half of all respondents continued the conversation in Catalan, suggesting to me that I'd made myself understood.

Conclusion: you do not have to become fluent in Catalan to enjoy the language in its social setting. In Barcelona you can get by without ever speaking Catalan. Even in the surrounding rural areas, where the wounds of Franco's prohibition of Catalan have never completely healed, people from outside of Spain are made to feel at home even when speaking *Castellano*. However, using a rudimentary Catalan, even with a poor accent or badly conjugated verbs, tends to enhance rapport with the people of Catalonia.

This chapter concludes with a few important phrases in both Catalan and Spanish. It is highly recommended that the visitor in Barcelona make an effort to learn either or both languages. Before going to Barcelona, you should attend a continuing education Spanish course in your home country. I say Spanish because in many places outside of Catalonia it's much more difficult to find a course in Catalan.

Once in Barcelona, you can find inexpensive courses in Catalan taught by highly professional language specialists at any neighborhood branch of the Centre de Normalització Linguistica de Barcelona:

phone: (34) 93 412 55 00
fax: (34) 93 412 15 50
e-mail: cnib@mx2.redestb.es

They have a whole menu of in-person and media courses. I recommend the general, in-person classes, for language is a social system, more easily learned in a group. Trimesters for these courses begin in October, February or July.

If a formal class is not possible, these centers also have facilities for self-learning, home study with occasional meetings, courses on CD-ROM, and specialized courses for your business.

Catalan courses are also available at the university. Contact the Secretaria del Servei de Llengua Catalana, maite@sic.ub.es or by mail to:

Gran Via de les Corts Catalanes, 585
08071 Barcelona

Spanish courses for foreigners are offered at:
Escola Oficial d'Idiomas de Barcelona
Av. de les Drassanes, s/n
08001 Barcelona
Phone: (34) 93 329 24 58
Fax: (34) 93 441 48 33
and:
Universitat de Barcelona
Gran Via de les Corts Catalanes, 585
08007 Barcelona
Phone: (34) 93 402 11 00

Languages are like species. The more we have, the richer our planet. Every foreigner who studies Catalan is helping to preserve a great living language.

A Few of the Most Strategic Words and Phrases in Catalan and Spanish

English	Catalan	Spanish
Hi	Hola	Holá
Goodbye	Adéu	Adiós
I'd like …	Voldria	Quisiera

(This is a polite way of asking for anything you need. Just add the noun after the verb!)

Where is…	On és…?	¿Dónde está…?
I'm looking for…	Estic buscant…	Estoy buscando…
How much is…(cost)	Quant val…?	¿Cuánto vale…?

Excuse me…	Perdoni	Perdón
Please	Sisplau	Por favor
Thank you (much)	(Moltes) gràcies	(Muchas) gracias
You're welcome	De res	De nada
Can I…?	Puc…?	¿Puedo…?

(Followed by an infinitive)

Beyond these highly strategic phrases, lists of words have little value, unless they are complemented with motivated language study, including verb conjugations and key vocabulary in context. Vowel sounds are a little more complicated in Catalan than in Spanish, but the shortening of vowel sounds in unaccented syllables resembles what English speakers already do unconsciously. English speakers can pretty much wing it with the consonants, in both Spanish and Catalan, by pronouncing them softly.

Spanish vowels each have a single pronunciation:

a = **ah** as in f**a**r
e = **eh** as in m**ea**sure
i = **ee**, slightly shorter than in m**ee**t
o = **oh**, slightly shorter than in pr**o**nounce
u = **oo** as in r**oo**t

Catalan vowels **a** and **e** are pronounced the same as in Spanish when they contain a written accent, but unaccented vowels are shortened in the form of a *schwa*, like the pronunciation in English of the final letter of panorama. The Catalan **i** is the same as in Spanish. The accented **o** is the same as its Spanish counterpart, but an unaccented **o** is similar to **oo**. The **u** is pronounced as in Spanish.

Space does not allow for an outline of regular verb conjugations in these two languages, but a practical list of those present tense irregular verbs most frequently used (pages 56–57) should be carried around like a crib sheet to get you through the day.

Not only do these few verbs account for a very significant portion of all verb use, but since they have all-encompassing, generalized meanings, they may be used to substitute for more specific, targeted verbs. Thus we can say "I **go** to Barcelona tomorrow" instead of "I **travel** to Barcelona tomorrow," or "I **am** a doctor" instead of "I **practice** medicine". These few irregular verbs save the day during the initial stages of the language learning process. When speaking a foreign language in this get-the-job-done-no-matter-how mode, we risk sounding infantile. But it would be more childish to not communicate at all. The verbs we'll outline are the same old suspects: to be, to go, to have, to be able to (can).

We first list the subject pronouns. In all charts, the Catalan language appears first, followed by Spanish, and then English.

1. jo	yo	I
2. tu	tú	you
(familiar, informal, used with friends, family)		
3. vòste	usted	you
(formal, used in business, commerce)		
4. ell, ella	él, ella	he, she
5. nosaltres	nosotros	we
6. vosaltres	vosotros	you
(familiar plural)		
7. vòstes	ustedes	you
(formal)		
8. ells, elles	ellos, ellas	they
(masculine and feminine in that order)		

In both Catalan and Spanish, the verb ending tells the listener who the subject is, so the speaker need not use the pronoun, unless there's a need to emphasize. Verb conjugations are now listed in the same sequence so as to match the above pronouns, but note that there are *only six different endings*, since **you** singular takes the same conjugation as **he/she** and **you** plural takes the same ending as **they**.

ESSER	SER	TO BE
(as a characteristic or identity, from "essence")		
sóc	soy	I am
ets	eres	you are (familiar)
és	es	you are (formal)
		he/she is
som	somos	we are
sou	sois	you are (familiar plural)
són	son	you are (formal plural)
		they are

ESTAR	ESTAR	TO BE
		(as a condition, location, from "state")
estic	estoy	I am
estàs	estás	you are (familiar)
està	está	you are (formal)
		he/she is
estem	estamos	we are
esteu	estáis	you are (familiar plural)
estan	están	you are (formal plural)
		they are

Note the difference between
és catalán (he is Catalan), which expresses identity, and
està cansat (he is tired), which expresses a condition.

Sóc professor (I am a teacher), which expresses identity, to *Estic amb els estudiants* (I am with the students), expressing location.

ANAR	IR	TO GO
vaig	voy	I go
vas	vas	you go (familiar)
va	va	you go (formal)
		he/she goes
anem	vamos	we go
aneu	vais	you go (familiar plural)

van	van	you go (formal plural)
		they go
TENIR	**TENER**	**TO HAVE**
tinc	tengo	I have
tens	tienes	you have (familiar)
té	tiene	you have (formal)
		he/she has
tenim	tenemos	we have
teniu	tenéis	you have (familiar plural)
tenen	tienen	you have (formal plural)
		they have
PODER	**PODER**	**TO BE ABLE TO**
puc	puedo	I can
pots	puedes	you can (familiar)
pot	puede	you can (formal)
		he/she can
podem	podemos	we can
podeu	podéis	you can (familiar plural)
poden	pueden	you can (formal plural)
		they can

Vocabulary Acquisition

Both Catalan and Spanish have a large number of cognates with English (words that are identical or similar to English). Nearly all English language words ending in –tion and –ity, for example, will be easily recognized and then used (and most words derived from such cognates will also be identical to or resemble English).

| condició | condición | condition |
| universitat | universidad | university |

We're talking about hundreds of important words we can immediately assimilate. Other words without such a happy similarity should be learned within the context of meaningful sentences and then soon recycled in other useful sentences before you've had the chance to forget. Rote memory of vocabulary has proven to be an unsuccessful strategy for most second-language learners.

The French Connection

People with studies in elementary Spanish and French can approach Catalan vocabulary by triangulating. When a new word pops up in conversation, try to relate the sound to either Spanish or French.

Numbers run the gamut of possibilities between French and Spanish. *Zero* is the same as Spanish and looks like English. *Un* (masculine) and *una* (feminine) look and sound like Spanish while resembling French. *Tres* is the same as Spanish. *Quatre* looks like French but is pronounced halfway between French and Spanish. *Cinc* looks a lot like both French and Spanish but is pronounced in Spanish phonetics. The numbers seven and eight, *set* and *vuit*, lean heavily on the French side of the pronunciation border. My favorite numbers are nine and ten. Their initial letters follow both Spanish and French, but otherwise they have a distinctly Catalan lilt: *nou* (noh-oo) and *deu* (deh-oo).

Many words straddle the line between French and Spanish, such as the word for kitchen: *cuina* (koo-eena), which begins like French (*cuisine*) and ends like Spanish (*cocina*). The first-person pronoun that means **I** is another example: French *je*, Spanish *yo*, Catalan *jo*, with the **j** being pronounced as in the French and the **o** as in Spanish. *Paraula* (word) has the final **a** from Spanish (*palabra*) and the isolated **l** from French (*parole*).

When French and Catalan began to take separate roads, it seems as if the French, in an off-road vehicle, took a misty side road in the direction of obfuscation, with numerous unpronounced letters. Catalan, on the other hand, chose a straighter, more well-marked highway, in the direction of obviousness. Consider the –tion words from English (already mentioned above for their providing of hundreds of "free" cognate vocabulary words even before we begin studying Catalan). Referring again to the English word "condition", we find that it has the same spelling in French, but the French do not pronounce the final **n**. The Spanish do indeed pronounce the final **n** in *condición*. In both Spanish and Catalan, the **c** replaces the **t** in the middle of the word, in order to more faithfully represent the true pronunciation of the word. So the English and French "condition" has a letter **t** that doesn't get pronounced as we would expect. The French cling to the final **n**, for no reason it seems, since they don't pronounce it.

In Catalan, *condició* reads and sounds like an editorial correction of French. In this and all other cases of –tion words, in Catalan what you see is what you get. Ditto for the word for "bread": *pa*. The French write it *pain* but when they say it, they don't pronounce the final **n**. The Catalan *pa*, sounding much like the French *pain*, may not taste as good as the French version, but sounds exactly the way it looks, as if it were an editorial correction of the French spelling, in order to make our task as language learners less "painful". Long live the Catalan language, for letting us see what we hear.

Sitting in a cafe with our friend Barbara (from Catalonia, with a Catalan mother and French father) and exchanging practice in English (for her) and Catalan (for me) was the equivalent of a gourmet linguistic recipe. When a new word in Catalan emerged, she could compare it with either French or Spanish, depending on what it most resembled, or simply give me the English equivalent if the Catalan went astray from French and Spanish.

None of this should imply that the Catalan language is derived from Spanish and French. (When someone tells me that my wife looks like Sally Field, I respond that Sally Field looks like my wife.) One could equally assert that French and Spanish are derived from Catalan.

The International Language

When eight-year-old Alec Smoley from the United States moved with his parents to Barcelona because of his father's new job, he had two new languages to confront. It was not easy for him at school, especially when at play with the other children, for he could not say what he wanted to do, and he was bewildered by the strange sounds coming in his direction. At the time, it was not much consolation for Alec to hear people say that children learn foreign languages quickly. Alec had the next day to deal with.

Sensible adults cope with a foreign language situation because we know that people are simply not going to speak the way we do. If we get lucky, we find another adult in our new country that has learned to speak English. But foreign children are less likely to have learned English, and a child like Alec must wonder why everyone is speaking "different" when he's never before experienced any communication problems.

As the only foreigner on his team, Alec found a way to communicate with his foot, before he could speak Spanish or Catalan.

Parents in Barcelona would do well to find an athletic activity for their children. Alec's mother, Kathy, became a "soccer mom". His father Dave had coached soccer in the United States, which gave Alec a head start at becoming accustomed to Barcelona's number one sport. Alec still had to adjust to the social Darwinism on the field, for with U.S. soccer a budding sport, young players receive lots of nurturing by their coaches and teachers, unlike their counterparts in other countries. But as the only foreigner on his Catalan soccer team, at least Alec had found a way to communicate with the other kids: with his foot. Soccer had become Alec's language of transition.

As the world's most popular sport, soccer is an international language. Foreigners who can dribble, pass and shoot have a way of integrating with the locals before learning the language of the country, and this is especially true in a place like Barcelona, where soccer is the grand sport, with such profound social and historical underpinnings.

In preparing for your stay in Barcelona, if you feel uncomfortable in a classroom repeating verb conjugations, perhaps you should go out to the athletic field and sharpen your soccer skills. In this way, you can become part of the team long before you've learned the local language.

CHAPTER THREE

GETTING AROUND
A Moving Experience

"It is a heavenly promenade, probably the best I know."

—James Michener's reference to Barcelona's Las Ramblas, from *Iberia: Spanish Travels and Reflections,* chapter on Barcelona

Getting around Barcelona seems too easy and mellow to need further explanation. The subways are comfortable and strategic, the trains run well, bus drivers are friendly and courteous. Bicycle paths are found along many primary arteries, you don't even need to take a taxi to the airport thanks to the fine train service available from various stations throughout the city and suburbs, and walking is sublime. Single, multiple-ride discount tickets for reasonable prices offer various transportation combinations (subways-buses, subways-trains-buses, etc.) so that ticket counters are only occasionally used, and when they are, the service is genuinely helpful.

This chapter would end right here, were it not for Barcelona's hidden obstacles against getting around. Let's confront the pros and cons of each type of transport.

WALKING WITHOUT GAWKING

Barcelona friends advised me that the best way to go is *a peu* (on foot). People who know the health value of taking brisk or long walks but have seen such activity as an uninviting task will be rewarded in Barcelona by scenery so dazzling that any effort to propel yourself is forgotten.

But the same beauty that brings us out to the street becomes the major obstacle, at least to the healthiest forms of walking. There are simply too many attractive sights, all functioning as visual impediments. The body wants to continue but the eyes act as brakes.

I've been practicing a new art form: the technique of walking past Gaudi buildings without gawking, but then the obstacles of other brilliant modernist architects like Domènech i Montaner must still be confronted along the way. Impossible to walk north on Laetano without being drawn, by a sensorial force a block off the path, to the audacious Palau de la Música, and then becoming paralyzed by its superimposed but unified styles: Moorish, Gothic, modernist, and the structured playfulness of Domènech i Montaner himself.

Such modernist architecture seems in complicity with human obstacles, especially on Las Ramblas and in the Gothic Quarter.

The Ramblas is supposed to be for walking, but people-watching triggers pedestrian traffic jams. The Gothic Quarter offers no relief. Just when you find a clear path in an uncongested alley in the Gothic Quarter or other parts of old Barcelona on either side of Las Ramblas, you are led to mysterious dead ends or seductive switchbacks, in one of the world's most incredible surviving man-made mazes. This is hardly a place for walking as

Author comes out of Metro station, gets swept into teachers' demonstration.

an exercise in fitness, and if you are walking for more practical reasons, like getting to an appointment, choose a different route.

Through the l'Eixample neighborhood, congestion diminishes, but the octagonal street grids mean that the pedestrian walks an extra twenty or thirty percent compared to an automobile going in the same direction in a straight line. The fitness gained from the extra distance at the forty-five degree corner detours is lost with frequent stops for traffic lights.

Barcelona is far from its radical, revolutionary past, but protest marches are frequent, and the pedestrian never knows when he or she will bump into a congested demonstration, as happened to this writer one Sunday noon. I got out of the Metro and all paths were blocked. Someone stuck a poster in my hand, the crowd began to move, and there I was, swept by the flow, defending public education against privatization.

On other Sundays at certain plazas, the pedestrian will meet up with *sardana* dancers and gravitate towards their concentric circles. (See Chapter 9)

The best place for an unimpeded brisk walk is the boardwalk, from La Barceloneta beach up the coast, but here you risk getting bowled over by a rollerblader or being sidetracked by the aroma of seafood coming from a boardwalk stand.

With eye-trapping Gothic facades, boulevard mimes and musicians, bewildering labyrinths, road-blocking protesters, rollerblading daredevils, and corners crowded with pedestrians who religiously wait for the stoplight to turn green, walking in Barcelona is never dull but rarely fast and steady enough to make revolutionary improvements in physical fitness.

CYCLING

Major thoroughfares such as La Diagonal and the boardwalk now have fine bicycle paths. Theoretically the cyclist has the right of way to any major attraction in Barcelona. But in reality, cyclists must beware of human obstacles along the way; Barcelona inhabitants often use the bicycle paths as sidewalks.

Bicycles may be rented at Un Menys (93 268 2105, at Carrer de l'Esparteria) or Chez Escenic (93 221 1666, on Avinguda de la Marina 22) at the equivalent of approximately five dollars per hour, with per-hour rates declining when the rental extends beyond the first hour. Long-stay residents should seriously consider bringing their own bicycle or purchasing one in Barcelona. Most

Metro and train lines allow the transport of bicycles within, during non-rush hour times.

EASY RIDING

A trip on either buses or subway costs 150 pesetas, but a ten-trip card (T-1, valid for bus and Metro) can be purchased at any subway station for not much more than half that per-trip cost, the peseta equivalent of more or less US$6). The per-trip cost descends even more with a 50-trip ticket, valid in the turnstile for no more than 30 days (T50/30 for the peseta equivalent of approximately US$25). Tip! By paying for these tickets with your visa or mastercard in the payment machines near ticket windows, you get the closest thing to the current exchange rate and evade the commission of moneychangers.

Bus

Bus drivers are generally courteous with foreigners and gracious in giving directions. Bus lines extend to parts of the city where the Metro doesn't reach, and aesthetically, a bus window has a better view than a subway tunnel. At any bus stop, the line numbers are accompanied by maps of the stops, so in a minute and eleven and two-fifths seconds, the newcomer with a city map will be able to choose the right bus. Traffic in Barcelona, while congested during rush hours, is more fluid than what we'd find in Paris or London. But frequent bus stops, even in non-rush hour surface trips, make the bus less practical than the speedier underground Metro.

Buses begin running between 5:00 and 6:00 in the morning, about every ten or fifteen minutes, and service terminates at about 11:00 pm, but night buses (*nitbusos*) take over, running every 30 to 45 minutes until about 3:00 am. Plaça Catalunya, the city's active womb, never stops delivering buses to all parts of the city.

A *Bus Turistic* costs about 2,000 pesetas for a day, with lower per-day costs for a two-day ticket. Such a ticket allows the short-term visitor unlimited trips, with stops at most of the major tourist sites. A long-term visitor will have little use for this bus, unless you choose to live in the suburbs and make only occasional incursions to the city.

Bus riders will miss the array of musicians and beggars who ply their trades in the underground.

The only real obstacle to bus travel is that the nearest bus stop rarely has the bus that is going exactly to your destination. Given that the buses are so much more attractive than the Metros, I've often said to myself "who cares?" when the bus I've found is going somewhere else. As long as it's going in the general direction, I board it anyway, and simply change my itinerary to make my connection elsewhere. Some of the anecdotes in this book refer to places I would have never discovered had I taken the Metro rather than the bus.

I've done some self-searching about the bizarre instinct that has me hopping on buses with little or no premeditation: the way a hen chooses a nest, or the way certain animals are attracted by bright colors. While modern, the subways are rather drab. From a bright red city bus, one can see the Barcelona sun flash upon the sea, the glistening mosaic tiles on modernist buildings, and bustling plazas.

Subways

The subways remain a more practical form of transportation. Some stations are adorned with attractive mosaic artwork. But mainly, the trains get you where you want to go, and fast. You can't get lost in the Barcelona Metro even if you try. Signs point the way, and from the platform, maps tell you the direction and the stops of the next train. A computerized monitor, found in many stations, counts down the minutes and seconds until the arrival of the next train, and usually gets it to within 20 seconds of perfection.

There's no charge for changing from one subway line to another, but the distance through pedestrian tunnels that connect the different lines is considerable when compared to the Paris or New York underground's. Seats on Barcelona Metro trains seem larger and more comfortable than their Paris or New York counterparts. Plaça Catalunya is the main nest station for the Metro, with lines 1, 2, 3, and 5 stopping there, and line 4 within walking distance.

It's easy to hop into the Barcelona Metro without paying, but when uniformed checkers stop you and you don't have your ticket stamped from the turnstile, you'll be fined 5,000 pesetas.

Obstacles for Metro users are few, unless you are elderly or handicapped. Only line 2 is accessible to the handicapped. If stairways are an issue, senior citizens or the disabled will find it easier to use buses. As with the bus system, the Metro stops running at about 11:00 pm on weekday nights. Given that Catalonians have such late dinners, especially in the summer, after leaving from a dinner invitation you may find yourself walking home, or heading for the nearest night bus. On Fridays and Saturdays, underground hours are more liberal, with trains running until approximately 2:00 am.

In Paris and New York, one convenience for subway users is the chance to get some reading done during the trip. I once wondered why there are so few book readers on the Barcelona Metro compared to New York and especially Paris. But then I tried to read a book myself. I soon realized that Barcelona subway rides are too short to be used as an office-on-the-way-to-the-office and more appropriate for haiku poetry.

Other Trains

Regional and suburban trains were once a nostalgic image of the Third World. Wicker seats, almost always worn and torn, noisy shaking and clacking, and tired faces are my sensorial recollections of such trains. We once lived in a building above a train line in a Barcelona suburb, and the building would tremble every seven minutes as a train passed by in either direction.

Now, such suburban and regional trains run in muffled grace. They have comfortable cloth seats, the people in them seem more cheerful, and they even beam in the music of baroque string quartets, the taste of a RENFE technocrat. Such trains now take you to beachside communities to the northeast or southwest of the city, and most strategic, to the airport. At this writing, a trip from Arc de Triomf, Plaça Catalunya or the Sants station to the airport on the regional RENFE (Spanish railways) line is only 330 pesetas: about two dollars, with a slightly higher price on Sundays and holidays. The trip takes only 20 minutes from Sants, 25 minutes from Plaça Catalunya, and 27 minutes from Arc de Triomf. Just purchase your ticket at the ticket window, then consult one of the boards for your next train, time of departure, and track. (If you have time to spare, there's a bus between Plaça d'Espanya and the airport (EN and EA) for only 140 pts. That will give you more than an hour to see every detail along the way.)

Ferrocarrils de la Generalitat de Catalunya (FGC) is yet another transportation alternative, depending on which city, town or suburb you are headed for. These and the RENFE suburban and regional train stations are part of the transportation complex at certain core Metro stations, among which, Plaça Catalunya and Sants Estació are the most conveniently located.

Automobiles

With one-way streets ribbing the city grid, traffic flows quite well in Barcelona. But parking is hard to find, and like other European cities, Barcelona tends to favor the pedestrian and user of public transport. When living in Barcelona, we had chosen not to own an automobile. However, many of the beautiful medieval villages and Pyrenees nature reserves are not accessible by train or bus, so people who enjoy such weekend trips may find it strategic to own a car, keep it garaged during the week, and use it for pleasure excursions and emergencies. Within the city, a motorcycle is more practical, especially since it does not often rain in this region.

Highways and roads are more than adequate. In fact, foreign business people surveyed on what they like and dislike most about Barcelona gave the highway infrastructure their best grade; 62 percent were satisfied with the highway and road infrastructure while only 6 percent were not satisfied.

Both new and used automobiles are advertised in the Motor supplement of the biweekly *Primeramà*, found at all newsstands. Most classified ads are placed by private sellers, while space ads are from dealers. For used cars, dealers often advertise "certified inspection by an independent enterprise," "12 months guarantee with highway assistance included," "free checkup after 2,500 kilometers," and "personalized financing".

Taxis

A green light on the roof and/or a "lliure" (free) sign within the windshield means a taxi is in service and available. In the equivalent of pesetas, taxis cost somewhat less than a dollar per kilometer, plus an initial fee and extra charge for baggage or late hours. Taxi cars adapted for the handicapped can be phoned at Radio Taxi Movil (93 357 7755) and Barnataxis (95 358 1111). It's easy to find a taxi outside airports, train stations, and around the primary plazas.

THE BRIDGE OF DISCORD

It was one of those times when I'd chosen a bus instead of the Metro, and ended up about 500 meters away from my intended destination, on the other side of a pedestrian bridge that crossed what looked like a freeway, the extension of La Gran Via, on the northeast side of the city, the Sant Martí district. There were signs painted on cloths which hung from the windows and balconies of high-rise apartment buildings lining the freeway on either side, all of them declaring Pont No Semáforo Si (Down with the bridge, up with a traffic light). I stood at the foot of the bridge and asked the first person who came by, a middle-aged woman, if the signs were some sort of protest against the freeway.

"Don't call this a freeway," she said. "No one ever approved any law to change it to a freeway. They built the bridge and now they're going to have to take it down."

The shoemaker on the same side of the bridge had his own version of the story. He looked up from behind his counter as he put the last buffs on a pair of shoes.

"The bridge is bad for business on both sides. People from the other side just don't want to climb up the steps or the ramp and cross over here. You see that the bridge extends far past the street. It's an extra walk. Senior citizens, parents with small children, and just about everyone else would rather have a regular street crossing the Gran Via. This is their community."

The shoemaker pointed to a poster on his window, which pictured a new and longer bridge.

"That's the project of the Ayuntamiento (Town Hall). We've been having demonstrations against it every Thursday. What we need is a stoplight."

A similar version opinion was expressed by the baker on the other side of the bridge. One of the customers in his bakery, an old-timer, former policeman, overheard my questions.

"We're on an island," he said. "Sant Martí should be one community, but they've split us into two."

Life on the outskirts of the city, Sant Martí style, is not seen by the tourists. Dull high rises and ill-kept town centers have no Gaudi buildings, nor Picasso museums, nor Gothic Quarter. What they do have, and are struggling to maintain, is their sense of community. The high rises, freeways, and shopping centers are impersonal, but here and there, a bar becomes a public hangout, a bakery a warm place to greet neighbors, a shoemaker's shop a place to announce the next meeting or demonstration, and a collectively-run continuing education center, a community refuge where residents can learn a new skill, prepare for university exams, or simply engage in lively discussions on literature and art. The absence of street gangs may have something to do with this tenacious community spirit.

I went back over the bridge to the Sant Martí Ayuntamiento and found a city planner.

"Surely," I said, "you must identify with what the neighbors have been telling me. Or is there another version to the story?"

"On the record I can't make any statement on the subject, but between you and me, we are trying to resolve the problem. There are politics involved, different interests that need to find a bridge [a poor metaphor], but in the meantime, a plan has been submitted to take the Gran Via below and have a pedestrian walkway at ground level, as part of an extended Rambla."

Without declaring any opinion, the city planner's projected demeanor and tone of voice seemed to empathize with the local residents.

"It doesn't look like we're going to get what we need," said a young woman with a child at the foot of the bridge. "I have to cross with my son twice a day, and it's not easy. Sometimes I just don't feel like coming over to this side. I think the Ayuntamiento and the Generalitat each have their own interests, and we're caught in the middle" [or caught on either side of the freeway, she should have said].

"The Gran Via is not a freeway," the woman echoed.

"But a traffic light would slow down the flow of automobiles," I said. "You might have a lot of angry drivers."

"Come back here during the rush hours," she said. "The traffic is backed up anyway. This is not a freeway."

There's a certain drama about getting around in Barcelona's outer neighborhoods, beyond the tourist core, where most of the immigrants and low-income families are obligated to live, for economic reasons. Amazingly, public gathering places in such neighborhoods have held on with determination, and visitors who stray from the center of town might be pleasantly rewarded.

AN ALTERNATIVE

Within Barcelona there are many self-contained communities, with all the facilities, amenities and entertainment potential to keep a resident happily on foot, on the streets around his or her apartment. City Hall has fomented self-contained neighborhoods by placing branches of key institutions within walking distance of most residential districts. Local Ayuntamientos, branches of business aid organizations, and adult education centers are all found within one's preferred neighborhood.

My choice was Gràcia, within walking distance of various Gaudí buildings and Parc Güell, with every type of commerce along the main avenue, Gran de Gràcia, and on side streets as well: a produce market and health food store at the Llibertat Plaza, and cleverly decorated cafe-bars around the intimate plazas of Virreina, Sol, and Rius i Taulet, narrow and intimate streets that favor the pedestrian and discourage automobile traffic, and branches of all the major banks. Each plaza in Gràcia is the scene of its own annual festival, with some plazas holding various events during the year.

If there's something you need and can't find, you can post a free advertisement in the local cafes. Ma-and-pa restaurants dish out home-cooked food at an affordable price, while a few upscale spots satisfy gourmet lovers. Several of the bars offer music performers with no cover charge. Political activists fight for various causes and make their presence felt by selling newspapers and holding forums. Vestiges of Barcelona's traditional activism have coalesced in Gràcia.

A self-contained neighborhood like Gràcia simplifies getting around, and reduces the maintenance aspects of life to a human scale. People can live a similar "local" lifestyle in other neighborhoods, depending on their persuasions. The point is that when adopting such a neighborhood, the strategy of getting around becomes manageable. You get to know the local bartender, storekeeper, flower vendor, photo developer, and you become a regular, an insider. This is a style of life that fits with the traditions and organic reality of Barcelona.

It would be impossible for one writer to actually live in multiple neighborhoods, but in preparing this book, I was able to live in two neighborhoods and frequent a third one regularly, covering three types of scenarios: inner city, outer city, and suburb. The self-contained, human-scale strategy worked well in all three places, even the suburb, which for some of its residents was becoming a bedroom community. In all three scenarios, the time required to use private or public transportation was reduced, and getting around was simplified.

When I did need to use the trains or buses, it was easy riding.

CHAPTER FOUR

FINDING A PLACE TO STAY
The Gleaming Tower of Pisos

"He explains to us that the situation is difficult, that there's more demand than supply, and vice versa, and that we should not harbor any illusions. He urges us to renounce the deceptive binomial habit of equating price to quality. He reminds us that life is no more than a highly regarded valley of tears."

—Extraterrestrial narrator's paraphrase of real estate agent speaking to a group of interested buyers, from *Sin Noticias de Gurb*, by Eduardo Mendoza

Among the few factors most frequently mentioned by foreign entrepreneurs as drawbacks to doing business in an otherwise glowing view of the Barcelona business scene was "the high running cost of real estate", according to a survey conducted by

KPMG Consulting. But a similar response might be elicited in surveys conducted in New York and Paris, and rents and property costs in Barcelona are significantly lower than what we would confront in the other two mentioned cities.

For newcomers in search of housing in Barcelona, the word is *piso*, which means apartment (literally "floor"). If your luck or timing is not good, you may have to settle for a *piso* in a *torre*, meaning high rise (literally "tower"), which may be good if your *torre* has a balcony view of the sea.

For renting a piso, the system is simple. Visit a real estate agency, called an *inmobiliaria* (or *immobiliària* in Catalan), tell the agent how many square meters you are looking for, what neighborhoods you would accept, and how many bedrooms you need. They will then let you know what they have available, tell you the amount of rent you'll need to pay, and if you express interest in any of these apartments, take you to see them.

Tip! To save hopping from one *inmobiliaria* to another, simply visit the Colegio Oficial de Administradores de Fincas, at Mallorca 214 (phone: 93 451 02 02), where they will "enter" the characteristics of the piso you are looking for and the price you are willing to pay, and print out a list of apartments that qualify, with the real estate agent for each apartment listed. They will ask for feedback on the places you visit, since they want to weed out the *timos* (or "teasers"), which are ads planted to get you to visit a realtor, only to discover that "the apartment you want is no longer available, but we have a nicer one for you at a higher price".

The reason this *inmobiliaria* system works so well is that someone pays for it: you, the renter. The commission or finder's fee for the apartment you agree to take is one month's rent. Experienced apartment dwellers in Barcelona have told this writer that they prefer to bite the bullet and pay the hefty commission since what they get in return is dependable service. We too decided to go this route. Given that Barcelona apartments are relatively less expensive compared to our North American experience, we felt we could absorb the commission cost.

But there are ways of scoring a direct hit on an apartment and bypassing the middleman.

- The least dependable method is to choose the neighborhood you like and comb the streets for posted advertisements hanging on the building where the apartment is available or on bulletin boards at local cafes. A significant percentage of these ads take you right back to a real estate company, so a lot of effort may be wasted in taking down numbers, calling, and getting the bad news.

- For students and youth, there is the Habitatge Jove, within the Secretari General de Joventut, Oficina del Programa Habitatge Jove (*Jove* refers to "youth"), Calabria, 147, phone: 93 483 83 92. Here you will find a data bank of pisos for youth between 18 and 35 years of age, as well as opportunities for sharing pisos, living with families, and university dorms. You pay no intermediary, and renters' insurance comes free. Increasingly, young adults are finding it more difficult to afford paying the rent, and end up either staying with their family until they marry or sharing a piso with other renters.

- Purchase a copy of the biweekly *Primeramà* at any newsstand, and take out the supplement called *Inmobiliaria*. Here you will find ads for rented pisos, listed in alphabetical order by the name of the neighborhood. Some ads specifically state they do not want to hear from intermediaries. Space ads are taken out by *inmobiliarias*, but classifieds are for free. (Some may have been planted by the real estate companies.) If you can find an apartment this way, you'll save the one-month finders' fee, but private landlords will usually be quite demanding in asking proof of your income and requiring security deposits. You can also place an ad in *Primeramà* stating that you are looking for a piso to rent. Expect calls from the agencies, unless you specify that you do not want to do business with third parties.

77

In general, you'll be asked for a month's *fianza* (deposit) and perhaps two months if you're renting a furnished apartment. According to several real estate agents interviewed for this book, as well as phone calls in response to ads, furnished apartments are not that much more expensive than unfurnished, although we found this to be true mainly in theory, since the availability of furnished apartments is limited.

Prices in some prime locations are as follows. In Gràcia, you can probably find a 2-bedroom for a maximum of 70,000 pesetas (less than $500). In l'Eixample, expect to pay between 70,000 and 200,000 (well over $1,000 a month) with the most expensive along La Diagonal. In chic residential neighborhoods with a view, such as Pedralbes, rents go higher yet. On the other hand, in funky La Barceloneta, near the beach, you can find a cramped 2-bedroom apartment for as low as $250 a month. Forget about the Olympic Village, also near the beaches. It's full, and renters not only plan to stay on, but consider themselves immortal.

Agents tell me there's a difference in preference among potential foreign renters. The Americans tend to seek comfort and parking facilities. The Germans are more demanding about the physical condition of the apartment. The English seem to be more willing to conform to the market. (That's *their* opinion.)

We've used the 2-bedroom apartment of approximately 70 square meters as a yardstick. Obviously the smaller you go, the cheaper, and it works in the opposite way if you're seeking 3 bedrooms or more, since space is at a premium in this city which is boxed in by mountains on one side and the sea on the other. Americans accustomed to a bathroom for every bedroom should prepare themselves for the good old days when people in a family actually shared the use of a bathroom.

If you're bold enough to look for rental apartments without inspecting them, try e-mailing one of the *inmobiliarias* that specialize in renting *pisos*:

Fincas Calvet: info@fincascalvet.com
Fincas Martret: terbesl@finquesmartret.com

In general, Mediterranean cultures prefer doing business in person. However, those that announce their e-mail are certainly encouraging a response. Potential renters who know neither Spanish nor Catalan might consider sending an e-mail in English. If the *inmobiliaria* scurries to find someone who can respond in English, then you're probably looking at a very motivated realtor.

APARTMENT SHARERS

Singles who have arrived in Barcelona may wish to explore alternative housing. Of the 88 pages in a typical *Primeramà* supplement, only one is dedicated to apartment or house sharing, listed under *HOSTES I VIVENDES PER COMPARTIR*. Some are actually individual rooms to rent within larger residences with kitchen privileges and shared use of bathrooms. Others offer a private bathroom, meals, and other amenities. Yet others include sharing the whole piso: *us del tot el pis* in Catalan. (Most ads are in Spanish but an important minority are in Catalan.) Many of these opportunities are sex- or age-specific, so a woman professor may prefer, for example, to rent to a nonsmoking woman. There's a certain degree of risk in searching for a piso to share. Future convicts in search of a new cellmate do not announce their status when advertising.

Occasionally there's free rent available, with strings attached, such as one which required the tenant to be present between 10:00 pm and 7:00 am, six nights a week to help a handicapped woman in case of necessity. In house-sharing opportunities, utilities are included. Such rentals run from between $150 and $300 per month. The rent may seem proportionally high in comparing with the independent piso rentals, but you're getting utilities paid for, furniture, and other amenities.

79

If responding to an ad for a bargain rental arrangement, be prepared to present as much proof of financial solvency as you would with an ordinary rental.

TEMPORARY LODGING

Short-term visitors who need no apartment or long-termers who want a place to park their luggage while seeking a piso will need a comfortable place to stay. Fortunately, hotels and their variations such as hostels and *pensiones* are less expensive than their counterparts in the industrial world's major cities. A 1998 survey of prices of 4- and 5-star hotels for business travelers, by Eurocast, listed Barcelona as the least expensive, compared to Milan, Paris, New York, Amsterdam, London, Frankfort, Tokyo, and Moscow.

At the other end of the economic spectrum, one can find a spartan but clean hostel room for less than $20 a night, depending on the season. The decor is not avant-garde Miró in these places, but when the human factor kicks in, including personal attention from the ma-and-pa-and-son-and-daughter owners, congenial TV rooms, and meticulous cleanliness, this option becomes more attractive. The prototype of such places is the San Medín in the heart of the Gràcia neighborhood, Gran de Gràcia 125 (phone: 93 217 30 68, fax: 93 415 44 10), Metro Fontana.

A happy compromise between the bottom and top ends are 2-star hotels in the $35-to-$60 range. Would you believe you can find such prices at a hotel with two dining rooms designed by the great modernist architect Lluis Domènech i Montaner, with a fresco by the fine painter Ramon Casas? This hotel with a history is called L'Hotel España, and is located at Sant Pau 9, in the El Raval neighborhood within a few steps of Las Ramblas (phone: 93 318 17 58, fax: 93 317 11 34), Metro Liceu. We got to know the place quite well because visiting friends were staying there, and it looked better than home sweet home: large, anachronistic rooms and very friendly service.

Keeping in the historical-artistic heritage and in the upper end of the middle range hotels, for between $70 and $100 a night, depending on the season, you can stay in the house where Miró was born, a nineteenth century building in the heart of the Gothic Quarter, now the 3-star Hotel Rialto.

Hotel seekers can scan other choices by visiting the website of the *Gremi d'Hotels de Barcelona*:

www.barcelonahotels.es

and if you see something you like, reach them through e-mail at:

gremihotels@cambrabcn.es

The alternative for the hostel crowd is:

www.gencat.es/jov

PURCHASING A HOUSE OR A PISO

Newcomers who prefer purchasing rather than renting their residence are advised to time travel back to pre-Olympic days and purchase whatever you can get. However, even the best of realtors do not provide this service. We had an opportunity to purchase a piso back then with a balcony view of the Mediterranean Sea, but we failed to act. Today, I become penitent and self-flagellating every time I pass that same building. I ask the nearest pedestrian to cane me. No haunted house could bedevil me more than that piso.

But today, Barcelona still offers value in the realm of property. Begin with the *Primeramà* supplement, "Cases & Nova Vivenda". You'll have a choice of numerous realty companies. In most of these companies you can find an agent who speaks English. The agency will provide free counseling on the legal aspects of foreigners owning property in Barcelona and the Catalonia region.

It is still possible to find older houses of character within the city, for prices that, relative to Paris, Manhattan, or London, are reasonable. In researching this book, I found one in an attractive residential neighborhood with two floors, four bedrooms, a sitting room, colonial windows and a wrought-iron balcony for $250,000. On the other end of the spectrum, one can find bargains in pleasant nearby towns within 20 kilometers of Barcelona by train. In the seaside town of El Masnou, on the Meresme coast, only 15 kilometers to Barcelona with trains every 20 minutes (round trip fare of about two dollars), I found an 85-square meter piso with a balcony view of the sea for $125,000. Pisos in older buildings of the gentrified Gràcia neighborhood can be purchased for less than $100,000.

The best strategy is to rent an apartment and get to know the city and the region quite well before purchasing a private residence, so this is not the place to get into the details of purchasing a piso. However, you can do some preliminary "window shopping" over the Internet by visiting realty websites:

SASI at www.sasi.es

IBUSA at www.ibusa.com

Don Piso at www.donpiso.com

The perception of availability and cost of Barcelona housing is very much relative to the origins of the foreigners in search of a residence. In a lifestyle survey of foreign business people, housing earned the least favorable grade among the various categories of quality of life, with 24 percent of those surveyed expressing satisfaction with Barcelona housing and 23 percent expressing dissatisfaction. Yet statistics flatter Barcelona in the realm of quality-price relationships, when compared with other European capitals.

Ads for the sale of pisos resoundingly outnumber those for rentals. Many realms of Barcelona life have been privatizing. Evidence that apartment owners outnumber renters is found in the lack of public laundromats, as compared to Paris, where renters outnumber owners and laundromats abound.

THE OCUPAS

With housing privatized, it is no wonder that a large brigade of disaffected young adults find it so difficult to find affordable housing. At this writing 150 buildings are occupied by squatters, nicknamed *Ocupas*. Most of them are young adults. Some are of working class background and simply do not have the income to afford a decent apartment. Others are middle-class and, for whatever reasons, want to leave their parents' home and live on their own.

Walking through a crowd of Ocupas can be intimidating. One sector of the Ocupa community seems to be in a body-piercing competition. The silent majority of the Ocupas are not so obviously identified. When Ocupas are being dislodged from an occupied building, they organize militant demonstrations.

I decided to get a better feel for this subculture and visited an Ocupa social club, an occupied building in the Gràcia neighborhood. Colorful murals decorated the walls, most of them unfinished. The hall had a bare wood floor in dire need of sanding and varnishing. The Ocupas were gathered in a Dalíesque way at a bar, with one man behind the bar and the others on stools or standing around. Most of them wore ragged clothing, and bizarre bangles emerged from the ears, noses, eyebrows.

I had been told that the Ocupas consider anyone who pays their rent as an accomplice to the system, so I was fully prepared to be either ignored or kicked out. From my barstool I listened to flamenco guitar music in the background. The shelves behind the bar were empty. The bartender was munching on sunflower seeds, one at a time.

He and the woman on the barstool next to me were quite pleased to engage in conversation. For a half hour we chatted about housing in Barcelona, and the low-paying jobs for young adults that did not allow enough income to pay the rent.

"We just do what we have to," concluded the bartender, who invited me to come back for their entertainment, and was interested in practicing English with me.

No one is living in this building, so the ocupas *occupied it and converted it into the social center.*

The next day, a friend and I decided to participate in an Ocupa demonstration. The march, accompanied by loud chants against banks, realtors, and anyone else with money, turned onto a main street. I asked my friend, "Do these guys have permission to march?"

"Are you joking? It would go against their ideology to ask the enemy for permission."

"Do you support them?"

"I support the need for affordable housing, but I don't support their methods."

I soon found out what he meant, as a few of the more energetic Ocupas leaped to the side of the march, armed with cans of spray paint, and began to epoxy political graffiti messages on banks, billboards, and other enemy establishments, signing with "Okupas".

If the police were to arrive to break up the demonstration and make arrests, I'd be in for a good eyewitness story, with a free pass to the lockup. I'd seen police wagons in the vicinity of the plaza where the demonstration began. Things were getting ugly, and I figured that the Barcelona police would be ready to defend property owners against the desecration.

"You think the police will break this thing up?" I asked my friend.

"No, they stay clear of these things, but I think I've seen enough. We gave our moral support, but we don't have to support their tactics. I think it's time to split."

We left the march and went to a nearby bar. The next morning, everyone in Gràcia could clearly see that the "Okupas" had temporarily occupied the neighborhood. The first rays of the Barcelona sun shone on black graffiti messages like "Housing Yes, Speculation No".

CHAPTER FIVE

MAKING A LIVING
Bread from Stones

"We have the work ethic, a sense of duty. We're more Calvinist than the rest of Spain."

—Barcelona business advisor

"From stones, the Catalan extracts bread."
(El catala de les pedres en treu pa.)

—Local proverb

Spain has a higher unemployment rate than most European countries, yet suffers such a scarcity of labor that the government has referred to the need for 45,000 new immigrants in the year 2000. During the Spanish colonial period, Spain went abroad for cheap and free labor. Today it's easy to bring the labor to Spain. North African immigrants do their adopted country a favor by coming to do jobs that Spaniards do not want to do, in an atmosphere in which anti-immigrant sentiment occasionally flares to the surface.

The rate of unemployment is high when compared to the standards of North America, the United Kingdom and Japan. But between 1995 and 1998, unemployment in Spain went down from 15.13 percent to 10.91 percent, according to optimistic official figures. Barcelona is flattered by such statistics. In the same period, Barcelona's unemployment rate eased down from 10.52 percent to 7.48 percent.

Like the housing scene, Barcelona's work situation is privatized to a greater degree than in cities like Paris or New York where the working class is more enfranchised: more home owners and fewer renters, more private entrepreneurs and fewer employees. Only 6 percent of the city's labor force is unionized, which means fewer and smaller demonstrations or marches than up the road in Paris, for example. Barcelona's anarchist and leftist labor history, so dynamic up until the Civil War, is largely a thing of the past. Without fanfare, local government business promoters attract foreign investment with the promise of labor stability.

But there are local nuances in labor customs that mask some of the roots of the region's working class. Unlike their French counterparts, Spanish truck drivers are more likely to own their own trucks rather than work for a company. But the Spanish drivers are still beholden to the enterprises they ship for. As private owners, they are paid by shipment, and receive no social benefits, which means it is in their interest to work excessive hours to earn enough to pay their bills and improve their economic situation.

Many Barcelona teachers cite what they perceive as a world trend of gradual privatization of education, which they fear will create a two-tiered system in which economically privileged children receive a better education. Unionized teachers march to defend public education.

As the society privatizes, an increasing number of traditional working class jobs are picked up by opportunity-seeking immigrants, most of them economic refugees. Ask most folks in

Catalonia and they'll encourage the stereotype that they are the hardest-working people in Spain, often with overtones suggesting that people from central and southern Spain would do well to learn the work ethic of the Catalans. Never mind that immigrants from other parts of Spain arrive in Catalonia to engage in strenuous manual labor that the locals choose not to do.

This is but a glimpse at the Barcelona work world that the newcomer will confront. In essence, those who wish to make a temporary or permanent home have three alternatives for earning a living in Barcelona: finding a source of income from their home country, finding a job in Barcelona, or starting a business.

CREATIVE SOURCES OF INCOME

Staying out of the work market and self-designing one's sources of income has its advantages and disadvantages. If you come from the United Kingdom, North America or Japan, your national currency will have significant buying power in Barcelona and it will be financially advantageous to find a source of income from your country of origin. The cost of housing, restaurants, hotels, and services is considerably lower than what it would be in the countries mentioned.

This means that newcomers can afford to stay in Barcelona with less income than they would require at home, and need not be so demanding, salary-wise, in the international freelance employment they seek. In theory, freelancers can arrange for the bulk of their income before arriving in Barcelona. A compendium of possible freelance income from abroad is beyond the scope of this book. A few examples will suffice.

For one who knows the business world, it is possible to do some groundwork for a corporation with aspirations of setting up a branch in Barcelona. People with an education or teaching background could do research on Barcelona's bilingual education system for think tanks or teachers' unions in their home region where bilingualism may be a potential alternative. Freelance writers and photographers have several major themes available: how the city is balancing its contemporary architecture with its modernist and Gothic traditions; the polemics regarding the uses of Catalan and Castillian in different layers of the society, with the repression of Catalan as historical background; the expanding Barcelona business scene; Barcelona's football history as a social phenomenon.

Freelance work can also be obtained creatively within the city. There is the Villa del Arte collective of artists, for example, most of them foreigners, who have pooled their resources to rent a gallery in the Gothic Quarter and make their living from the sale of their paintings and sculptures. In order to do this, they take turns staking themselves outside the gallery and personally inviting passersby into their "free exhibition".

"Why don't you come in and check it out?" says Bert, one of the artists. "It's painless."

Since many foreign tourists pass by on the way to the plaza by the cathedral, an important market comes within a few meters of their artwork on a daily basis.

People in the arts are willing to cruise in survival gear in exchange for living in Barcelona. Foreign musicians and performing artists gravitate to Las Ramblas and Plaça Catalunya to practice their art in public scenarios and pick up some spending cash from passersby. During various stays in Barcelona, I've found Andean musicians making good money playing and selling cassettes on Plaça Catalunya and a Finnish sax player with money-making gigs in clubs who felt comfortable playing a handmade reed instrument on Las Ramblas.

Other foreigners I met in Barcelona have hustled up gigs as private English teachers. One can approach personnel departments of international companies that want their employees to learn English, or advertise for free in *Primeramà* and on cafe

89

bulletin boards. Cafe owners and bartenders in neighborhoods off the tourist path are remarkably friendly in allowing patrons and strangers alike to post ads.

With the financial advantages of freelance work comes the disadvantage that you will have a lower degree of social interaction than you would on a more formal job or in running a business.

GET A JOB

Work is a major topic of conversation among Barcelona inhabitants, and a more formal job allows for the type of solidarity that exists within the work force. But the unemployment statistics cited above are deceiving, for within highly competitive professions where unemployment makes a greater impact, it is more difficult to find a job.

Citizens of European Union countries, Iceland and Norway, need not have a visa in order to obtain a legal job. But should they be staying beyond the normal three months, they must immediately apply for a *carta de residencia*. An employer offering you a job will help you take care of the paperwork. Otherwise, be prepared to go through the process step by step. By consulting with your local Spanish consulate *before* you leave for Barcelona, you will know exactly which documents are required, and where to take them. (See Chapter 8)

For those who are not from an EU country, this process is virtually impossible without the help of an employer. There's a classic Catch-22, as illustrated from my personal experience. A language institute wanted to hire me and asked for my working papers. I told them I had none. I went to the government and asked about getting papers. They told me I would need an employer to do the paperwork, consisting of verification that the employer could not find local help with the same skills. I went back to the employer, and they told me such a procedure was too much of a hassle, unless I could promise a long-term commitment. Without knowing for sure how I would adapt to this institute's teaching philosophy and working conditions, it would have been dishonest for me to make such a commitment. I had enough freelance work to keep my family fed, so I let it drop.

If you teach for an English language institute, more than half of what your labor produces will go to the institute, and since the work is usually part-time, you won't be eligible for social benefits. But if you can handle mature learners from the business world, some institutes will be especially interested in you, for their best paying clients want the utmost professional teaching service.

Whatever your craft or profession, you have a long shot chance to find a job before you arrive in Barcelona. Simply place a free ad in the *Demandes de Treball* section of *Primeramà*. You're allowed one free ad every other edition, and ads must be from private parties. Phone: 902 508 508, fax: 93 508 55 01. Your ad can be in either Spanish or Catalan. Make sure your response number has the correct international country and city codes.

STARTING A BUSINESS

> "One Catalan starts a business. Two Catalans organize a corporation. Three Catalans form a choral society."
>
> —a local saying, as quoted by James A. Michener

Newcomers with professional skills, and financial backing to go with them, may be better off forming their own institute or service company than working for someone else. For any business start-up, among the plethora of Barcelona business organizations, there is one that is set up with you in mind: Barcelona Activa.

Barcelona Activa is a local administrative unit with branches in different districts of the city, whose goal is economic promotion, entrepreneurial support, innovation and the creation of employ-

91

ment. (Though it's more well known for its support of business entrepreneurs, Barcelona Activa also has a division that provides free orientation for people in search of a job.)

As soon as you know you want to start up a business, visit the head offices of Barcelona Activa, on Llacuna Street in the Sant Martí neighborhood (Metro Glories). The receptionist will set you up with a personal appointment. Be prepared to wait as long as two weeks for an appointment. Business people planning on a short preliminary trip to Barcelona can set up such an interview by fax or e-mail. In my case, I needed an appointment before my research went off on wasteful tangents. I handed them a letter explaining my urgency and they called me two days later with an immediate appointment time.

My first impression of the Barcelona Activa headquarters was the dominance of the Catalan language in conversation, written materials and posters. That was fine with me, as I was interested in practicing my Catalan, but I was concerned that the people who should benefit from my research would be confronting a language barrier.

When I arrived at my interview, two representatives, Laura Salom and Mario Rubert, both insisted on speaking English. Not good for my practice of Catalan, but great for potential business people from abroad.

Barcelona Activa's three main personalized programs, all free of charge, are: (1) help to entrepreneurs who have an idea for a business, including a business plan service, help with paperwork and red tape, and consulting; (2) training programs dealing with starting a business and following through; (3) the ODAME program to help women start a business.

Barcelona Activa also has a highly regarded "business incubator" program. There's a fee involved here, but it's well below the going price for equivalent services in other countries. The business incubator provides space for a company to begin operating, with subsidized rent and shared e-mail, fax, receptionists, consulting, and training. Such collective services are intended to foment cooperation among companies. The incubator lasts a maximum of three years. There is also a virtual incubator, interactive, through the net.

In comparing all the options for newcomers to make a living in Barcelona, the business option is the friendliest. I was made to

Barcelona business conference scene.

feel at home at Barcelona Activa, and quite tempted to switch over from my freelancing to a more entrepreneurial mode. A seductive array of business conferences adds to the entrepreneurial ambiance.

SECTORS

I was particularly interested in which business sectors were projected to have the most promising future in Barcelona. Ms. Salom and Mr. Rubert obliged me by enumerating what they believed to be the most business-friendly and rapidly emerging sectors: knowledge, new technologies, personal services, culture and leisure, and security were the five most important of their top sixteen.

More traditional sectors still thriving are: automobile manufacture, textiles, pharmaceuticals, and publishing. Mr. Rubert proudly emphasized that for all its defense of the Catalan language, Barcelona was also the number one city in Spanish-language publications.

FINANCIAL AID

Barcelona Activa has a special arrangement with banks for more attractive interest rates for its clients, and a financing search mechanism as well. Special aid is channeled to smaller business projects in the realm of 20–30 million pesetas, or US$120,000–200,000.

GETTING STARTED

Caution! There is no need to read what follows unless you are seriously considering starting a business in Spain. If this category is not of primary interest, skip ahead to "Adjusting to Barcelona's Business Scene".

Great pains have been taken to extract what is the most salient and practical information from the general base of Spanish law for potential business people. This information is intended as an introduction, and before any steps are taken, if you still want to go ahead with your business, you should get a free copy of the booklet *Investing in Barcelona*, available through Barcelona Activa.

Three legal entities have some say in your business. Newcomers may be frightened by having to deal with the Spanish government (*Ministerio de Hacienda*), the *Generalitat* (the autonomous government of Catalonia), and the *Ayuntamiento* (city hall), but the division of responsibilities of these three entities is quite simple. The Spanish government is the primary licensing and taxing organism. The Generalitat deals with such rules as business hours, days off, holidays, etc. City Hall only gives you a single form to fill out, which deals with the *Quota Municipal*.

INVESTING IN BARCELONA

Northern Spain, both Catalonia and the Basque Country, has traditionally been attractive to foreign investors because of its exceptional communication network with other European countries, with Barcelona as a privileged center of operations.

Foreign investors must follow specific rules of the Spanish government involving registration of the investment and the movement of funds to and from Spain, such as an "export report" to verify that the value of the contribution covers the investment made.

Legal forms of investment include: business through a local agent, a representative office, branches, business enterprises, and joint ventures.

Foreign companies and individuals often use local agents to sell their products in Spain, as a preliminary stage for establishing their own production or service facilities. Since all legal implications and risks under such an agreement are the responsibility of the company that requires the agent's services, a carefully drafted agency agreement should cover all major issues such as prices, discounts, payment terms, and advertising, and should be written to cover a predetermined period.

A representative office is a simpler option, with the responsibilities of such an office reduced to the execution of market studies, contacting present and prospective clients, providing publicity, and other preparatory activities required by the parent company.

A branch office means that the corporation need not have its headquarters in Spain. However, for both exchange control and tax purposes, the branch is treated as an independent entity and is subject to the same rules as for a Spanish resident company. But read the fine print: liability is not limited to capital in Spain, but rather extends to the entire capital of the parent company.

Opening a branch in Spain requires a Notarial Deed, which must be formalized and registered with the Commercial Registry.

The next option is the "business enterprise", with five possible categories:

- Stock Company (*Sociedad Anónima, S.A.*), must be headquartered in Spain, in which shareholders are not personally responsible for the debts accumulated by the company: (a) form with certification from the General Commercial Registry, and a notarized Deed of Incorporation; (b) draw up the Bylaws of the company; (c) execute the Public Deed of Incorporation before a Notary Public; (d) pay the Stamp Tax (1 percent of capital stock) within a month of signing the public deed; (e) apply for a Fiscal Identification Number within 30 days of the formation of the corporation.

- Limited Liability Company (*Sociedad Limitada, S.L.*). This type of company must be located within Spanish borders, and may have no more than 50 investors, with a minimum of two investors. An S.L. company goes through the same five procedures as the S.A. to be officially formed.

- General and Limited Partnerships are more idiosyncratic, and nuances of such businesses will be explained to potential investors by the business attaché at any Spanish consulate.

96

- Joint Ventures are becoming more common even though there is no legal definition for such an entity. The formation of joint ventures between Spanish and foreign companies is increasingly prevalent because of the globalization of the economy and because such an entity creates important opportunities in the Spanish market for foreign investors.
- The most common type of joint venture is the Spanish Commercial Entity with Foreign Participation. This is the simplest form of joint venture. For this type of business, the Spanish government advises that one of the two investors should have majority rule, "avoiding the parallelization of business activities".

Rights of the Foreign Investor

Foreign investors are allowed complete freedom of action with the exception of certain clearance limitations and special circumstance authorization.

Foreign investors have unrestricted legal rights to transfer the following assets abroad:

- invested capital and the eventual capital gains from investment in Spain;
- dividends and profits arising from their investments;
- all capital movements arising from investments, including the transfer of funds to make the investment, and the remittance of dividends, profits and capital gains.

Investments are divided into different legal categories, including "direct investment" (foreign investor legally domiciled outside the territory of Spain), "portfolio investments" (including the purchase of shares in Spanish companies and other types of securities), "real estate investments" (which require prior clearance if the intention is a tax haven), and other forms of investments that include joint ventures, foundations, and cooperatives. The general rule for most investments is that they do not require prior administrative clearance unless they exceed 500 million pesetas or if the purpose is a tax haven.

Exchange Control Regulations

The Spanish government is authorized to prohibit or limit transactions or related payments by businesses and international organizations if they affect Spanish national interests in the realm of national defense, air transport, and radio and television.

The export of cash, bank notes and bearer checks in either pesetas or foreign currency is subject to prior declaration if it involves a sum that is greater than 5 million pesetas.

Corporate Income Tax

The general corporate income tax is 35 percent. The taxable base is modified by deductible expenses in the realms of depreciation and amortization, leasing contracts, reserves and provisions (such as third party liability provisions and doubtful debts), and other expenses, such as employee payroll (including directors' profit-sharing up to 10 percent), interest on commercial loans, and payments to registered pension funds. On the other hand, capital gains are generally added to business income.

Spanish and local government business authorities often mention that their tax structures are favorable to foreign business people when compared to taxes in other industrialized countries.

There is a more favorable tax base of 25 percent for income obtained without a permanent establishment, whose broad categories are described as:

- income arising from services, technical assistance, loans, work, or capital provided or used in Spain;
- income from securities issued by resident companies in Spain;
- income from property located in Spain;
- capital gains on the sale of assets located in Spain.

Nonresident companies owning real estate in Spain are subject to an annual tax of 5 percent on the cad astral (adjusted) value of the property, payable by December 31 of each year. This tax is deductible for corporate purposes.

Nonresident entities earning income in Spain are required to appoint a Spanish resident as a fiscal representative.

P.S. If you have read through this section without blinking, then you are especially qualified to do business in Barcelona!

ADJUSTING TO BARCELONA'S BUSINESS SCENE

Foreign business people operating in Barcelona are very positive about the city and its people, according to several surveys.

"When we established a campus in Europe," comments Robert S. Hamada, Dean of the University of Chicago's Graduate Business School, "we wanted to be in a city with a creative and innovative spirit, a business orientation and convenient transportation. Barcelona was our first choice and we are delighted that we now call the city our home in Europe."

Gerald Hines, chairman of Hines, a development company, was especially pleased by "a culture that reveres the old and applauds the new".

Reasons why businesses choose Barcelona vary from one source to another.

Transport

Some of the most frequent responses relate to the fine public and private transportation facilities and nearness of both port and airport. It is cheaper to transport products from the south of Europe to the north rather than the other way around. Barcelona has the largest container port in the Mediterranean. It is also the least expensive European capital as regards business travel.

Cost-performance Factors

Others revere the productivity of Catalonia, with 7 percent of Spain's population and 15 percent of its GDP. Cost-performance factors rate highly. Labor costs for each unit produced are 12 percent lower than in the United States (1998 statistic). One reason was that Barcelona workers had the lowest rate of absenteeism and defective products in all of Europe. Relatively low taxes and highly competitive utility costs add to its cost-performance record.

Fairs and Congresses

An indirect but still worthy reason cited by many interviewed business people was Barcelona's importance on the fair and congress circuit. The momentum from two previous world fairs plus the 1992 Olympic Games has helped Barcelona become the fourth most important city in the world in the organization of fairs and congresses.

Public Support of Private Initiative

Barcelona Activa is one example of the government's commitment to private enterprise. There is an intrinsic belief that innovative business will reduce the unemployment rate, and thus far this correlation has been corroborated in practice. The Catalan government along with cooperating institutions offers an 11-point incentives plan. Traditional, peripheral areas are now organized into "New Centrality Areas" of business activity.

In order of preference, the main criteria for enterprises choosing to operate in Barcelona, according to a survey cosponsored by Barcelona's Ayuntamiento and KMPG Consulting, are: (1) size and relevance of the local market; (2) quality infrastructures and services; (3) previous activities of the company in Barcelona; and (4) the city's positive geographic location.

Barcelona officials are quick to point out that real estate consultants Healy and Baker ranked their city number one in a 1999 report on Europe's top cities in terms of quality of life. Whether we are willing to accept such a ranking depends on whether we agree with the indicators, such as opera houses and golf courses, used by Healy and Baker. The fact that the city has three opera houses may not be the perfect indicator for a jazz lover, for example, but fortunately, Barcelona is also replete with jazz clubs and schools for performing musicians. The existence of 44 golf courses is fine for golf players who can afford the sport, but the city's bicycle paths and free beaches might be a more important indicator for Barcelona workers and foreign students alike.

Certain statistics are either good or bad depending on the eye of the beholder. Business promoters are proud to quote a 1995 International Labor Organization report that shows only 6.1 percent of the work force to have union membership. Seen from a different perspective, the low level of union membership may explain why Barcelona workers have longer workdays and shorter vacation periods than their more heavily unionized Paris counterparts.

To the credit of the Ayuntamiento and KMPG Consulting, great efforts were made to find out which factors, in the opinion of foreign entrepreneurs, needed improvement. Improvements called for by those surveyed, in order of importance, included: (1) the completion of impending infrastructures; (2) better fiscal treatment; (3) a greater recognition of difficulties created by bilingualism in company environments and activities; (4) greater work flexibility; and (5) the containment of real estate prices.

The Ayuntamiento survey uncovered certain areas in which more respondents were unsatisfied rather than satisfied. Some of these were "Help with Investment", "Financing Advantages", and "Research and Development Centers".

When asked questions in different ways, business people had different responses within the same categories. An overall view of areas of satisfaction and dissatisfaction, with satisfaction largely outscoring dissatisfaction, is now summed up as a handy reference:

Satisfaction:

Geographic location	75% (of respondents)
Quality of life	69%
Image of Barcelona	67%
Social climate	64%
Road networks	62%
Political stability	59%
Air communication	55%

Dissatisfaction:

Public help	47% (of respondents)
Policies of support for companies	43%
Labor flexibility	35%
Favorable land costs	33%
Alliances with local partners	29%
Attitude of local administrators	28%
Favorable financing	28%
Knowledge of languages	25%

Business people interviewed by this writer did not see much of a problem with the fact that Barcelona had two new languages to assimilate, while many of them found that they could operate in both *Castellano* and English. International schools have programs that encourage the learning of both Catalan and *Castellano* for their students. One U.S. businessman, a parent of children going to school in Catalonia, said, "I'm pleased my son can learn both Spanish and Catalan. We're aware that once we leave, he may never have the need to use Catalan again, but we also know that more languages expand the mind of the child. On the job, I get help from the employees with my Spanish."

Ultimately, making a living in any foreign city requires creative persistence. This book doesn't pretend to act as an employment agent. But Barcelona may be one of the easiest places to find a niche for both the artistically inclined or those with a business background. Barcelona has set precedents involving foreigners in its intimate history. Most locals will remember or are aware that foreigners fought bravely against fascism during the Spanish Civil War. During more contemporary times, foreigners have had a positive presence in many professions and sectors of society. The newcomer with a creative spirit, innovative ideas, and a friendly attitude will be well received.

Chapter Six

EATING
Salsa's Not Just a Dance

"The sauce costs more than the fish."
(Costa més la salsa que el peix.)

—Catalan proverb

Do the Catalans really work harder than the Castillians? Who knows? When a cliché is repeated enough, you begin to believe it. Another cliché may be nearer the truth: that in Catalonia one eats better than anywhere else in Spain. "Better" depends on your taste, and if you don't like garlic, almonds, olive oil, and eggplant, you may not be pleased by Catalonia's most typical sauces, which hold the secret of its food.

When you need a break from the brands of Catalan nationalism based on language or work habits, get involved with culinary nationalism. According to Vásquez Montalbán, "… cuisine has brought the last grand cultural wave to a city well stocked with restaurants and chefs, as much in traditional cuisine as in nouvelle or artistic cuisine".

With both sea and mountains, Catalonia is ideally placed for a variety of eating experiences. Much of this cuisine involves frying ingredients at some stage of the cooking process, with meats, egg yolks, oils, and other apparently unhealthy foods unavoidable. Health and diet researchers might find Barcelona an excellent research site. Everything that is supposedly bad for the health is combined with many items that are suspected to be good: olive oil, red wine, and above all, garlic.

As a nonsectarian vegetarian, I've developed my personal strategy for dealing with such eating contradictions. I limit my culinary excesses to one meal a day, usually a full-course lunch with red wine, some time after which I walk it off, or take advantage of the city's bicycle paths. The other extreme of my schizophrenic regimen includes spartan breakfasts and dinners involving whole grains, soy milk, and plenty of fresh fruit, with no refined sugar or cholesterol. This is not intended as dietary advice, and I expect that such a rationalistic regimen will be scorned by the experts in diet and health.

CATALAN CUISINE

Our friends Monse and Luis have explained, while preparing delicious lunches, that the secret of Catalan cuisine is in the sauces. One of Monse's favorites is *samfaina*, prepared with fried onion, tomato, garlic, red pepper, and eggplant. She adds whatever fish she is using half baked to the sauce, with the juice extracted from the fish replacing any need for water. When her sauces need thickening, she uses fried bread.

- Simpler than the *samfaina* is *sofregit*, the same formula as above without the red pepper or eggplant.
- *Allioli* (literally garlic and oil) is another of Monse's favorites. She prefers this sauce without the optional egg yolk or mayonnaise.

105

- Another Catalan sauce that comes out exquisite even in simple bar food is *picada*, which combines garlic, diced almonds and parsley.
- My favorite bar cook, Maria, prepares an especially delicious fish dish with *romesco* sauce, including tomato, diced almonds, olive oil and vinegar.

In Barcelona one has the choice between traditional Catalan food, an abundant variety of Spanish food, a limited number of international restaurants, and here and there, bars and quirky restaurants that prepare their own avant-garde recipes.

Some culinary adventurers will prefer to concentrate on Catalan dishes:

- One of the most complex, because of the different stages for adding each ingredient, is called *Suquet de Peix* (fish casserole). The end product is usually two varieties of fish chosen for their freshness by the cook, cooked in a complex sauce. One eats the fish while dipping bread in the sauce. The sauce includes toasted almonds, fried garlic and onion, fried and basted bread, a dash of fish liver, a spoonful of sweet pepper, another of flour, saffron, potatoes, and the natural juice from the cooked fish. Five minutes before the potatoes and fish are finished cooking in this sauce, the cook adds white wine, *aguardiente* (pure alcoholic beverage), and a mildly hot pepper called *guindilla* (cayenne family).
- *Fideuá*, a local form of *paella* cooked in noodles instead of rice. Squid, shrimp, sausage, red peppers, and other goodies can be added.
- *Sarsuela de marisc*, a rich fish stew with *merluza* (hake) and lobster, or other combinations. (If Catalonia had a catchall version of the basic "steak and potatoes" we know in North America, it would be hake and potatoes, or hake and rice. *Merluza* is the fundamental staple that gets you through the

week. It's inexpensive, can be baked, fried or grilled, and combines with a variety of sides.)

- *Escudella*, a meat stew with vegetables.
- *Fricandó*, juicy pork and vegetables.
- *Botifarra amb mongetes*, a complex sausage served with fried white string beans, or with *setas* (a rough-and-tough mushroom with a meaty taste).
- *Cargols*, a certain snail dish served with *conill* (rabbit) and red pepper.
- *Mar i muntanya* is a general term for various dishes that combine fish and meat.
- *Paella*. Everyone knows about paella, and the fact that it originated in nearby Valencia, once part of the Catalonia empire, where Catalan is still spoken today. By the letter of the law, paella is not from Catalonia, but the best paella we ever ate was prepared at home for us by a Catalan lady friend.

Dessert is always included on the fixed menu. A few highlights from Catalonia's extensive dessert list are dutifully noted. *Crema Catalana* is a type of light custard, known as *flan* in the Hispanic world, typically served as part of the fixed-price lunch. A more special treat is *Postre de music*, dried fruits (especially

107

figs and raisins), hazelnuts, almonds, all of this toasted into a delicious texture. *Natus con chocolate* is somewhere between mousse and pudding. A wide variety of pastries is also available, although these are usually consumed as breakfast or as a snack. Mendoza's extraterrestrial became hooked on *churros*, a fried pastry stick tasting somewhat like donuts but lighter in texture. Rather than a snack, *churros* may be eaten as breakfast with hot chocolate: *xurros amb xocolata*.

Some of Catalonia's most creative dishes are its salads. One of them is *escalivada*, which includes grilled red peppers and eggplant, with olive oil and garlic.

Even when snacking you can't get away from the garlic. A most popular snack is *pa amb tomaquet*, a slice of bread brushed in garlic and tomato, sprinkled with olive oil and salt.

BAR FOOD

If you are working in the city and don't go home for lunch, you have at least two hours to kill, so you might as well take your main meal. You'll want a comfortable place where you can kick back and relax, and eat well for a reasonable price. For around six or seven dollars (from 800 to 1,200 pesetas), you can get a worthy fixed-price lunch that includes two main courses, a dessert, and wine or other beverage.

Barcelona is bursting with the type of neighborhood bars that cater to just this type of person. For the newcomer, the strategy is simple. Try lunch at several bars in the neighborhood, and then stick to the one or two of them with the best food and service. Once you are seen as a regular, and it won't take long, you'll find they serve you better wine and more of the goodies in your stew. Bars where the waiters are also the owners are usually more humane than those with absentee owners.

Not being a meat lover, I needed a bar where the cook would go lightly on the meat and add more to the sides. By becoming a

Maria (with one of her regular clients) tends the bar she owns, does the cooking, and still has time to chat with her valued customers.

109

regular, I was able to intervene in the preparation of my lunches, asking Maria to go heavy on the eggplant or *setas* and light on the fish or pork.

The "regular-at-the-bar" strategy does not work for those who like their privacy and would prefer to eat lunch while reading the sports pages or business news. Once you regularly inhabit the same bar, informal relationships develop, conversations are ongoing, and you can pretty much give up reading your paper.

In more upscale designer bars, the ones which "compete" for the most artistic decor, the food is more expensive and elaborate, although probably not as bountiful. In such places you're more likely to find veggie dishes and bizarre combinations that cannot be ascribed any regional designation. The menu at slick, attractive cafe-bars like *Salambó* (in Gràcia) will please gourmet taste buds for only a couple of dollars/few hundred pesetas more than what you'd spend at the homey, funkier neighborhood bars.

RESTAURANTS

When it comes to restaurants, most travel guides drag out the usual suspects and list them in encyclopedic form, thereby taking away the adventure of eating out. Of more strategic value is a methodology for choosing a restaurant on sight. Here we present a three-point test in helping you decide to enter or pass.

- First and foremost, look at the food on diners' plates. The secret of Barcelona food is in the sauce. If what you see is dry, a slab of meat, for example, or breaded fish, you've not found one of the best chefs in town. What if no one is eating at the time? It means word-of-mouth publicity has backfired, and the place is not to be trusted. In this respect, an exception can be made for vegetarian restaurants, since Barcelona inhabitants do not flock regularly to places where they cannot eat meat or fish.
- You may not be able to judge a cook by his cover but the intrinsic value of a restaurant is sometimes found in its design.

Marco, to the right, working at Los Caracoles.

Subjectively I've felt that slick-looking restaurants that have hired a designer to create an atmosphere have less appealing and probably more expensive food than those with funkier designs done by or presided over by the proprietors themselves. In this art-conscious city, if restaurant owners have been actively involved in designing their site, they are more likely to have participated in creating a truly unique menu. Avoid places that look a little too slick.

• Arrive at off-hours when the servers have a chance to chat. If the waiters have worked at the same place for more than five years, it means tips have been good and/or they haven't gotten tired of the food, and/or they've been treated favorably by the proprietor: good reasons to stay on the job. When owners are sensitive to the needs of their help, it means they'll probably be sensitive to the tastes of their clients.

111

Barcelona's legendary Restaurante Los Caracoles passes the test on all three points, so don't give the place a demerit just because Richard Nixon once dined there. Marco, the waiter I interviewed, has worked here for more than a decade and has no desire to move. The waiters are well fed, and I was tempted to simply order what they were eating. Restaurante Los Caracoles is Barcelona's oldest restaurant, run by the same Bofarull family since 1835. Each of its different salons has its own design, but none of the ambiance comes from the drawing board of a marketing-minded designer. The jovial owner mingles with his customers, and sees his business as an art. Seafood is the specialty of the house, with their own brand of paella, but you won't be disappointed by *butifarra* (sausage) and *seta* (mushroom) casserole. You can enjoy a full meal for between $18 and $25, not bad when considering this is a top-end place. (Gothic Quarter, Escudellers, 14)

The other famous historic restaurant, whose theme design resuscitates its turn-of-the-century Bohemian past is Els Quatre Gats (The Four Cats), in a building by the great modernist architect Josep Puig i Cadalfalch. An à la carte dish here can run from $8 to $18, with a full-course meal more expensive. (Gothic Quarter, Montsió 3 bis)

For quicker and cheaper food, various alternatives are recommended. The less ornate bars offer the best *tapas*, small plates of saucy foods served at the bar to accompany drinks, for a dollar or two per plate, a Spanish custom. For quick and cheap food, in most neighborhoods you can get a well-served falaffel sandwich for not much more than $2. Several places in Gràcia, all called Equinox, offer falaffel and shawarma. Fixed-price lunch menus for 1,000 pesetas or less are ubiquitous. Likewise, here and there you'll find vegetarian restaurants with full fixed-price lunches. I never found one that was full. No use recommending one, for the chances of their remaining in business are limited. You get a good view and reasonable prices at the 9th floor cafeteria of the Corte Inglés department store on Plaça Catalunya.

FOOD SHOPPING

No matter how much we've tried, we've never been able to do our shopping in one place. For food shopping to be less an errand and more an outing, try the historic covered markets occupying whole city blocks or more. Mercat de la Boqueria, just off the Ramblas, is the prototype. But most neighborhoods have their similar markets, where you can go from vendor to vendor until you find the right produce with the right price. I've shopped at such markets in La Barceloneta and Gràcia, and have never been disappointed. Finding a regular vendor will make shopping more pleasurable, and most vendors will ultimately give you certain advantages once they know you'll be back, adding an extra piece of fruit or two, or making sure you've chosen the very best she or he has to offer.

At the historic markets, certain products are either not available or more expensive than at the nearby supermarket, where daily requirements such as milk, juices, pastas, and cereals are found in abundance and variety. Products vary from one supermarket to another. At one market, for example, I found packaged wholegrain crackers and cookies imported from Greece but could not find the same products at other supermarkets in the neighborhood.

On the perimeter of the quadrant around the historic markets, small health food boutiques fill a void in the food economy. The prices, as can be expected, are relatively high. But items like soy products and exotic grain cereals not available in most neighborhood supermarkets can be a healthy and tasty addition to one's weekly menu.

Compared to your country of origin, the relative cost of food varies from item to item. In the year 2000, food in general was slightly less expensive in Barcelona than it was in Paris, and a few notches less than in New York or Los Angeles, but you lost this price advantage at health food stores.

Vegetarians have never had it easy in Catalonia, but once

113

they've got their kitchen set up, they can self-cater successfully with an abundance of nutritious and satisfying products. The ubiquitous olives brighten up any plate, wholegrain breads are available at certain bakeries, packaged low-sodium and high-grain crackers and cookies at various supermarkets, fresh produce from the covered markets, with health food stores filling the gaps.

Eating adventures in Barcelona and the surrounding territory are unlimited. Some of the best cooking can be found in small cities and villages on the perimeter of Barcelona. Each neighboring place seems to have its own specialty. In nearby El Masnou and Alella, I found an incredibly delicious almond candy that I couldn't find in Barcelona, manufactured by a bakery called Francesch Pujadas. Don't use a guidebook. Take the risk and explore.

By chance I found one of the most remarkable restaurants in my whole career of searching for such places. In a town called Tiana I came across an old thirteenth century building, painstakingly restored by its owners and converted into the restaurant Mas Blanc. The specialty is cod in allioli sauce, the food is good, but most of all, the setting is the treat. You've got a small village, country atmosphere only 10 miles (16 km) from Barcelona. To get an idea of how old this place is, consider the window in the hall overlooking the cash register. This stone-framed window high above the entrance hall, reached by ladder, has built-in stone benches, for one person on either side. One of them (on one side of the window frame) was for the *doncella*, the young damsel who was being courted from below by her suitor. For the suitor to be nearer to his beloved, he would sit on a horse. The bench on the other side of the window frame was for the chaperon: the aunt, mother or *dueña*. Call this functional medieval architecture.

Purists will argue that electric lights and modern bathrooms ruin the atmosphere of the Mas Blanc restaurant, but I was pleased to use modern spoons and forks, and to be able to wash up in a well-lit bathroom.

114

Kathy Smoley

Savannah learns to eat calçots. *(Turn the page for more about them.)*

Kathy Smoley

Alec and his dad with calçotada *cook.*

Mas Blanc is one example. Look harder, farther up in the hills, and you will find home-cooked Catalan food in yet more primitive settings. To get to Mas Blanc, take a commuter RENFE train from Plaça Catalunya to the coastal town of Montgat. Either hike uphill about a mile or look for a taxi at the Montgat station.

THE *CALÇOTADA*

In country manors (*mas*) converted into restaurants, or at back-yard barbecues, one of Catalonia's great eating experiences is the *calçotada*. *Calçots* belong to the onion family and look like overweight scallions. They are grilled until they turn black on the outside and juicy within. Then the blackened part is slid off and the *çalcots* are dipped into *romesco* sauce. *Salsa* is not just a dance. It flows freely at a *calçotada*, where we are given bibs and are expected to use our hands, in an uninhibited eating experience, the vegetarian equivalent of a Maryland crab feast.

CHAPTER SEVEN

SHOPPING
Will Success Spoil Barcelona?

"Barcelona's a thrill when there's money in the till."
(Barcelona és bona, si la bolsa sona)

—Catalan proverb

During the final decade of the past century, Barcelona suddenly plunged deeper into the consumer society. The 1992 Olympic Games were the probable trigger for this inevitable transformation. The city always had great boutiques, but now shopping malls are vying to take over.

From the outside, the floating Maremagnum looks quite impressive. Its sleek modern design, with the marina yachts parked before it, is a symbol of triumph. Barcelona's port has been cleaned up. One arrives at Maremagnum over a continuation of the Ramblas, first passing by what used to be an extension of the seedy port, the *Barrio Chino*. Once the 42nd Street and Pigalle of Barcelona, the *Barrio Chino* is now a boring stretch of Las Ramblas on the way to a shopping paradise.

Like other *Centros Comerciales*, Maremagnum has no respect for the traditional three-hour mid-afternoon break, with commerce continuing from 11:00 am to 11:00 pm. Once inside, Maremagnum looks hardly different than other state-of-the-art shopping malls. You could be in Minnesota, Orlando, or Toronto.

It used to be that even iconoclasts who opposed the consumer culture used to enjoy shopping in Barcelona. The surprise element dominated, and personal service humanized the process. Now, the city has designed the Shopping Line, translated: "el Shopping Line" (Catalan succumbs not to Madrid but to the global culture), a pedestrian connection between the old port, Las Ramblas, the historic center of town, Plaza Catalunya, and l'Eixample with its posh commercial and financial row along La Diagonal. The city's tourist bureaucracy has conjured up the imaginative nickname: "Barcelona Ciudad de Compras" ("Shopping City"). A special bus line called Tombbus runs up and down the Shopping Line. Discount cards such as La Tarjeta Visitante Comprador and La Barcelona Card offer apparent discounts for the city's most prestigious stores.

Other malls beyond the Shopping Line seem redundant, until you visit them. Barcelona Glòries happens to be located across from what may be the most offensive traffic circle in Europe, the brick and cement wasteland of high walls called Plaça Glòries Catalanes. Suddenly a windowless mall with an open courtyard in its center looks better than its surroundings. But once inside, most of the stores are nostalgic reminders of generic suburban malls of North America. Headline: "Culture Gap filled by The Gap".

After such mallsville, traditional department stores like El Corte Inglés seem to be glorious defenders of a more authentic

Barcelona. Never mind that the massive, blocklike Corte Inglés architecture is an insult to Gaudiville.

Is this the end of Barcelona as we knew it? Will the medieval streets in and about the Shopping Line become hyperboutiqued to the extent that they function as an extension of the malls? Will ma-and-pa stores be able to keep their clientele? Will Barcelona's millennial coarse textures be manicured to adapt to the Global Consumer? Will the seedy characters of the seaport's gritty past lose their social relevance? Will personalized shopping as it used to be survive, with one-of-a-kind products popping up in the store just around the corner?

Tourists for whom this shopping line was conceived may just be the ones to help hold the fort and defend the authentic Barcelona. Many have come here to get away from their shopping mall existence. If visual imagery at all serves as evidence, most tourists continue to prefer the quirky boutiques over the globalized malls. Shopping alternatives still abound in and around Barcelona.

MA AND PA

Saving the day is the friendly service of neighborhood proprietors within the district of the Shopping Line, and especially in neighborhoods beyond the tourist core, including shops in the smaller periphery cities within 10 or 15 minutes of Plaça Catalunya by train, such as Badalona. Barcelona's historic commercial culture will probably save it from the global consumer culture.

Once again, the district of Gràcia becomes an exemplary prototype of "the old neighborhood", with photo shops, florists, newsstand vendors, grocers, lively cafe-bars. But even in an outer district like Sant Martí, clogged with dull high rises, I found shoemakers, bakers, realtors, cigar store vendors who could win awards for pleasant and friendly service. As one who is known for hating shopping, I now admit in print that I love shopping in Barcelona, where the most mundane errand acquires a touch of grace. Neighborhood businesses follow an approximate schedule of 10:00 am through 2:00 pm, reopening at about 4:30 pm and closing at 8:00. If shopping fatigued you in the morning, you have time to take a nap, and do it again in the afternoon.

The key seems to be the conjunction of two factors: the high percentage of proprietor-operated businesses and a culture in which personal and sociable service is the standard.

FLEA MARKET

Aside from your regular shops, Barcelona offers attractive shopping alternatives. *Els Encants* (The Charms) is a flea market currently located across from Plaça de les Glòries, where you can find just about anything you need, from appliances and bicycles to clothing and collectibles. A whole universe converges within a few acres of the city. Days and hours are Mondays, Wednesdays, Fridays and Saturdays (excepting festival days) from 7:00 am to 8:00 pm on sunny days, and one hour less on each end when it's raining.

Shoppers can find flea market bargains at Els Encants.

121

Manuel Iglesias

For quirky items, shop at antique fairs.

Antiques

For antiques, an alternative to Bulevard de los Antiquarios (Pg. de Gràcia 55) and Gremio de Anticuarios de Cataluña (Rselló, 233) are periodic antique fairs in nearby towns, announced in newspapers.

Once a week, Thursdays, the outdoor Mercado Gótico de Antiguedades decorates the plaza in front of the cathedral with interesting displays of goodies from the near and remote past. The city also has numerous stamp-and-coin shops and artisans' stores.

THE 7-POINT PLAN
(to Lower the Cost of Living and Raise the Quality of Life)

Anyone can cut costs by skimping on quality. The trick is to cut costs while getting better products and services, as several Catalan proverbs suggest can be done. At least 205 proverbs from Catalan culture sing the glories of *estalvi* (economizing or saving) and the folly of *malgastar* (waste). Here are a few ideas that apply specifically to Barcelona but may also be applicable in other European capitals.

(1) Currency Exchange

Use your credit card. If you are reading this past the year 2002 and are from a European Union country, you'll be dealing in the single currency, the Euro. Otherwise, be ready for steep commissions when changing money. The best way to circumvent gouging commissions is by making as many payments as possible with a credit card from your home country. You then pay up before the end of the month, as if you'd paid cash. Restaurants, supermarkets, pharmacies, and sites of daily commerce all take credit cards. When paying with a credit card, you get the closest thing possible to a fair exchange rate.

If you prefer to deal with cash, the best exchange rates, at *casas de cambio*, are often what seem to be the worst, as apparently poorer exchange rates don't have a commission charge. For large amounts of money only, you can do better at a bank than an exchange store.

(2) Banking

Shop around at as many banks as possible before opening an account. In this way, you are assured of getting the best possible interest rates and the lowest service charges. Should you decide to open an account in *divisa*, say dollars, go to the head branch of the bank (most headquarters are on La Diagonal), and before you open the account, make sure there are no hidden transaction charges.

It is very easy to open an account. All you need is a valid passport. In researching for this book, I visited 20 banks and with the friendly and meticulous service of the account officers, I never came away disappointed. Tip! For the most undivided attention, the best time to visit a bank is at opening time.

(3) Regular Shopping

If you need a product or service on a regular basis, it is best to use the same merchant, and always choose a shop in which the proprietor is on site. Once they know you, you'll receive certain perks. For example, at the photography store where I had photos developed, once the owner got to know me, he automatically redid those photos of mine that he wasn't pleased with, to add or remove light. He did this free of charge.

(4) Furniture and Household Items

Depending on the length of your stay, it may be better to get a furnished apartment. The longer you stay, the more feasible it becomes to purchase those household items you have not brought with you. Used furniture, lamps and other items are often of better quality than what you would find in a retail showroom. Needless to say, you will also pay less. You may find quality bargains at Els

Encants flea market. Otherwise, look under *LLAR I SALUT* in *Primeramà* for the items you need. Other sections of *Primeramà* advertise items like personal computers, bicycles, and tools.

For whatever item you need, if you doubt the validity of this strategy, visit a showroom first, and then compare the price of the used item you find. With a little patience, you will find just what you like for less than half the price. Especially in the case of furniture, lamps, and tools, accept only items that are of better quality than what you would have found in the showroom. Indeed, older furniture often goes up in value, while something you purchase new will suddenly be worth half as much once you've sat in it.

(5) Sales

New clothing, household items, and virtually everything else one would need go on sale twice a year at most retail shops and department stores in town. Winter sales: beginning approximately 7 January for two whole months! Summer sales: the months of July and August. With four months of significantly reduced prices, there's never a long wait until sale day.

(6) Transportation

Unless you have many family members traveling in a group, using public transportation is considerably less expensive than using a private vehicle. Gasoline is much more expensive in Catalonia and Spain than in the United States. Public transportation both within Barcelona and beyond is considerably less expensive than in most U.S. cities.

The devil's advocate will argue that many beautiful medieval villages and mountain campsites are only accessible by car. However, with a fraction of what you save by using public transportation, you can rent an automobile for your vacation. Many great places in Catalonia and Spain are reachable by train, including medieval Girona, the Dalí museum in Figueres, the Costa Brava (train or bus), Montserrat, Sitges, and some sections of the Pyrenees Mountains.

If you must own a car, you can keep it garaged for most of the time and only use it for holidays and emergencies, as many of our acquaintances do.

Those who use the subways and buses frequently can purchase multiple ticket cards at great savings. The more tickets on your card, the lower the per-ride cost. These cards allow you to bypass the ticket counter. You stick the card into a slot, it comes out stamped, and you pass through the turnstile.

(7) Preventative Health

European Union residents qualify for public health service. Other visitors should either purchase international health insurance, find a policy in their home country that covers them abroad, or purchase private insurance in Barcelona. Health care costs are generally less expensive in Spain than in northern countries. But the savings in health care come with intangibles that foster preventative health, such as a relatively warm, dry climate that allows for ample outdoor aerobic physical fitness activities. There's the lengthy boardwalk, beach and parks for walking and running, numerous bicycle paths, and swimming in the sea or at inexpensive public pools.

The jury is still out on the degree of effectiveness of preventative health dietary methods, but research points favorably to

126

garlic, olive oil and red wine (in moderation), all important staples in Barcelona, as active agents in preventing heart disease and fostering longevity. Barcelona's neighborhood markets offer a healthy array of fresh fruit and produce. High-fiber foods and whole grains are found in health food stores, and even in some grocery stores and supermarkets.

In Barcelona it is possible to live a truly enriching life without being rich. The cost of living is already more than a few notches lower than it would be in London or New York. Taking it from there, newcomers who still need to lower their cost of living should do so in a way that simultaneously raises their quality of life.

CHAPTER EIGHT

BUREAUCRACY
183 Days

"Everything is discussed and decided collectively."

—Montse Sanchez Aroca

During various periods in Barcelona's history, syndicalist-anarchist movements attempted to turn what we know as bureaucracy upside down and inside out, shaking loose all the heavy hands and legalistic minds until what was left was a consensus-based decision-making process that got things done when the heat was on. In the early days of the Spanish Civil War when the anarchists were defending the Republic against the fascists, the anarchists had a word-of-mouth system through which, from one moment to the next, everyone found out about an important gathering. Once arrived, the people spoke and a decision was made based on what was said. Everyone knew their roles, and the decision was then acted upon, immediately.

Those were heady days when people took things into their own hands, with visceral consensus organization skills that today we'd find difficult to reproduce. In isolated pockets here and there in Barcelona, this tradition survives. One such place is the La Verneda-Sant Martí continuing education school, an institution so successful it was written up in the *Harvard Education Review*. The ongoing drama at La Verneda-Sant Martí is the continuing extermination process against the fungus of any hierarchy that begins to fester within the organization. Administration and education policy is determined by collective discussions and consensus.

It can be safely predicted that newcomers arriving in Barcelona will be confronting more traditional bureaucracies during the adjustment process.

I entered City Hall (*Ajuntament* in Catalan; *Ayuntamiento* in Spanish) to visit with various officials to obtain information for this book. At the desk in the lobby, I presented my credentials and was given a badge, which allowed me to use the elevator and reach the offices on the upper floors. Following my interviews, I left an office and found myself in an upper floor hall with a spectacular picture-window view of the city. It was a partially cloudy afternoon, not ideal for a photograph but I took out my camera. Rooftops are like the private parts of a city. Even the taxi drivers and foot patrolmen who best know a city can pass through a lifetime without becoming acquainted with a hidden personality of their city, as it is seen from above. From here I had a close-up view of the top of the Gothic Quarter, much more intimate and unmanicured than what I'd seen from afar on the hilltops to the west. I snapped a couple of potential photos and left.

The following day, the clouds were gone and I decided to return to City Hall to take some improved photos. I approached the same desk, presented the same credentials, and explained to the same woman, who looked maybe like a chaperon or governess, that today's visit was much simpler. All I needed was a quick trip up the elevator to snap a few photos through the picture window in the hall. I wouldn't have to disturb anyone this time.

Yesterday I had been considered a journalist, today a voyeur. The chaperon at the credentials desk explained that her instructions were to not supply passes to photographers.

"I was just here yesterday," I said. "You let me up there."

"Of course I did. I remember you," she responded, and how could she not, since most foreign visitors do not stumble through a Catalan obstacle course when they could have pranced through in Castillian. Today was different, the chaperon explained, as I began to feel like a scorned suitor. "Why don't you go up that stairway and consult the head of security. They are the ones who can issue a permit. But I doubt that they will."

After a half-hour wait, a security official arrived. She looked more like one of the boarding school students than a chaperon, and my hopes rose accordingly. Surely she would see the difference between the spirit of the law and the letter of the law.

"We have very strict rules prohibiting anyone from taking photographs in the building. I think you can understand that."

"Yesterday, I was here with my camera and no one stopped me," I said.

"But yesterday, you were not *supposed* to take photos either. I'm sorry, I understand your purpose, but I have strict orders to enforce this rule."

"Do you want my roll of film from yesterday?" I suggested.

She smiled, and suggested I go to the top of Sagrada Familia, which is too high and far away from the neighborhood I was interested in.

I had been so accustomed to finding the loopholes in Barcelona's intimidating legalistic bureaucracy that I was totally surprised by the ultimate and final decision coming from a totally unintimidating security officer. In retrospect, I could have easily gotten around the bureaucracy by asking for another appointment with any other official in the building, and then taking out my concealed camera when in the hall outside the elevator.

If this had been my only experience with the bureaucracy, I'd have come away with the false notion that anyone who attempts to penetrate into the soul of officialdom is predestined to be turned away. But this was not the case. Time and again, once the technocrats and commissioners were aware of my intentions, I was suddenly escorted into a conference room and lent an interested ear. In Barcelona the medieval code from 1060, the *Utsages de Barcelona*, no longer acted as a barrier between the aristocracy and the public.

There is no particular rule for dealing with the bureaucracy, except perhaps the obvious: courteousness. However, Barcelona's split personality, belonging to a country (Spain) and a nation (Catalonia), requires that newcomers have a general awareness of which officialdom is the one they need on any given occasion.

First it must be known that City Hall is usually in the hands of the socialists (Maragall and Clos), while the Generalitat of Catalonia is the turf of the nationalist conservatives (Jordi Pujol). In 1999, Maragall attempted to alter this post-1978 balance by challenging Pujol for the governorship. Although Maragall got a few more popular votes in the final tally than Pujol, Pujol's conservatives gained the edge through pacts with smaller parties.

Under Pujol's leadership, Catalonia was able to capture a number of official functions typically in the hands of a central government, including local police, the education system, tourism, commerce, agriculture, health, social security, and culture. Even before you arrive in Barcelona, you will discover that Catalonia's tourism agencies around the world, rather than Spain's, are your best source of travel information for Barcelona. In the realm of taxes, this expanding autonomy allows Catalonia to collect more than what would have been considered a fair share of taxes by the former centralist government.

131

But long-stay foreign visitors will soon discover that most bureaucratic business will go through Spain and not Catalonia. Immigration and work papers are controlled by the State. For whichever visa you need, the place to go in your home country is the Spanish consulate. Remember the formula: travel information, the Generalitat; travel documents, the Spanish government.

Tourists from most English-speaking countries need only arrive with a passport, but laws and bilateral agreements change, so it's always sensible to phone the Spanish consulate in advance of travel to Catalonia.

Student Visa

A student visa requires a passport valid for more than six months, a formal application for the visa, three recent I.D. photos, a certificate that shows registration in a university with a minimum of 15 class hours per week, proof of financial solvency to the tune of resources approximating US$600 per month, a medical certificate proving there is no sickness that would threaten public health, and a psychological statement that the visitor will not be a threat to the public order.

Business Visa

The foreigner who wishes to open a business in Barcelona will be required to show a passport with at least four months of validity, four recent I.D. photos, a police report from your home country showing that you've been clean for the past five years, a medical certificate with the same prerequisites as those required for a student visa, but which also shows adequate health for engaging in a professional activity, and last but not least, an application for a work permit, to be stamped within Spain by the Barcelona delegation of the Ministry of Labor.

Work Visa

Official documents do not mention how long this will take, but one reliable source from within told me, off the record, to expect six months. The same requirements as above (valid passport, four recent I.D. photos, signed application form, police report, and medical certificate) are accompanied by what seems to be a Catch-22: a Spanish work contract which mentions your N.E.V. number, N.E.V. being a special work-visa related I.D. You must have this work contract stamped by the Spanish Ministry of Labor, Barcelona branch.

This means that if you are not planning on working "under the table", you'd better find your employer before you actually go to Barcelona. The employer is the one who will deal with the bureaucracy, on your behalf.

European citizens will have an obvious advantage in the working paper arena over visitors from non-European Union countries.

For any visa concerns, potential long-stay visitors in Barcelona would do themselves a great favor by asking for an interview with the Spanish consul in their home countries.

Tip! Once you become a resident, you'll be required to pay taxes. The magic number is 183 days. *Es consideren residents aquells que viuen en territori espanyol més de 183 dies a l'any.* (Those who live in Spanish territory for more than 183 days of the year are considered residents.) Remember that number when planning the length of your stay. If you stay beyond the 183 days, you'll need an NIE, which is a fiscal identification number for foreigners, obtainable from Oficina de Extranjeros of the Spanish State in Barcelona: Av. Marques Agentera 4; phone: 93 482 05 44.

BEGINNING AT THE HUMAN SCALE

It would be impossible for a book like this to anticipate each and every possible bureaucratic need of all its readers, but one important tip will save you time and help you through any procedures once you're there. It is always better to begin at a more intimate scale of operation. For example, if you go to the main *Ayuntamiento* on Plaça Jaume for any particular reason, they will probably send you back to your district city hall. Tip! The district *Ayuntamiento* not only offers services within the boundaries of the functions of City Hall but employees behind the counter know exactly where to send you if it turns out that the procedures you need are not within the jurisdiction of City Hall. In some district *Ayuntamientos* you walk right up to a counter, while in others you take a number and wait for it to be called.

In the procedural realm of doing business, the functions of City Hall (a simple fiscal form) and the Generalitat (laws on work hours and vacations) are not as important as the Ministry of Finance in the Spanish government, referred to as *Ministerio de Hacienda*.

Tip! A publication called *Guía de la Ciudad*, available in most bookstores, will have the updated list of bureaucratic procedures, and an encyclopedic repetition of what is in that guide is beyond the scope of this book. Here you'll find phone numbers and addresses for obtaining utilities (phone, electricity, gas, water) for your new apartment if the landlord does not already take care of this for you. The Colegio Oficial de Administradores de Fincas is your one-stop source for all bureaucratic questions referring to housing and utilities: Mallorca 214; phone: 93 451 02 02.

OFFICE HOURS

This can get tricky. Most places of official business are closed during the lunch hours, between 13:00 and 16:00. However, increasingly, offices are changing to a continuous schedule. Foreigners used to think they could arrive at any office in mid-afternoon, as they would in their native lands, only to discover the doors closed. Now, the big surprise is that you get there in the late afternoon, confident that you'll be attended to, only to discover that visitors are received on a continuous schedule from 9:00 to 14:00 or from 8:30 to 17:30. The best tactic is to phone in advance.

TAX REFUNDS

The I.V.A. (*impuesto sobre valor agregado*) or value-added tax is 7 percent for hotels and restaurants and 16 percent for consumer goods. Visitors who do not intend to live in Barcelona for more than three months will receive refunds on taxes paid for all purchases of more than 15,000 pesetas (approximately US$100) depending on the exchange rate at the time. With each such purchase, ask for a receipt or *factura* that states the amount of the I.V.A., which is usually included in the price of purchase, and the name of both seller and buyer. *Facturas* should be presented at a special customs window at the port of exit. The customs officer will hand you a stub, which you take to a bank at the site of departure in order to get reimbursed. Allow time for this process. If you get to the airport just before your flight, you might as well consider your I.V.A. expenses a tip to Spain.

MAIL

Postal service is best done from the post office itself, but I've been assured that yellow mailboxes on the street are just as sure a bet for outgoing letters. Stamps may be purchased in stores called *tabacs/tabacos*, or directly from the post office. You can't miss the central post office in front of Port Vell (Plaça d'Antoni López) open between 8:00 am and 10:00 pm (until 8:00 pm on Saturdays). Worldwide couriers DHL and UPS are at your service for urgent packages.

PUBLIC PHONES

It gets confusing since some phones take coins, others phone cards (purchased in increments of 1,000 pesetas from Telefonicaet), and credit cards, or some combination of the three. Phone cards may be purchased at post offices or tobacco shops. Once you are a regular at a bar, the phone becomes available for a lower cost than the phone booth. The Sants railroad station has a phone office open throughout the workday from Mondays through Saturdays.

INTERNET

Most phone connections will be fine for your modem, but NEVER plug in until you have reconfirmed that the connection is okay, with your landlord, hotel desk, etc. Internet cafes are found here and there, especially in the Plaça Catalunya-Ramblas-Maremagnum corridor, but user fees are steep. If you plan on frequent e-mail or Internet use, you might as well get yourself a computer or bring a laptop with you. Prior to your trip to Barcelona, you'll find many websites with practical information by surfing around. You can get to know the bureaucracy in advance by visiting the *Ayuntamiento* (www.ben.es) and the *Generalitat* (www.gencat.es), or for practical information, try www.deinfo.es/barcelona-on-line (general info) and www.infobarna.es (tourism).

ELECTRIC CURRENT

The standard is 220 current. Never plug a 110 V apparatus into a 220 socket or you will burn out the motor. Appliances using 110 V can be first connected to a transformer, with the transformer plugging into the wall socket. But one brief failure by a cheap transformer can ruin your 110 computer, shaver, radio, or CD player. Newcomers to Barcelona from 110 cultures should find appliances that work with 220 current before they depart for Barcelona, or buy new ones after arriving.

The incompatibility of flat-pronged plugs from North America with round sockets in Europe is resolved with simple adapters, purchased at any hardware store or even in some supermarkets, for the equivalent of a couple of dollars.

A BUREAUCRACY-FREE LIFE

Those who have a distaste for dealing with people behind a counter should try the following formula:

• Provide for an income from abroad.

- Rent a furnished apartment with utilities and phone included.
- Visit the Spanish consul *before* you travel, and have all your papers in order.

VIVA LA BUROCRACIA

Or try the opposite approach. In Catalonia and Spain in general, the friendliness and courtesy of people behind the counter is noteworthy and genuine. We're not talking about people schooled to flash a phony smile. Of course you'll find every variation within the human spectrum, but in general, it is a pleasure to deal with people in Barcelona.

So why not bite the bullet and decide to enjoy your bureaucratic encounters. With the Internet and other technological methods replacing human contact, one day you may look back with nostalgia at the great and simple moments in which a real human being provided services with a genuine smile. I suspect that Barcelona may be one of the last bastions in the world where direct contact between human beings is defended as a great tradition, no matter what "practical" alternatives become available.

— CHAPTER NINE —

ENTERTAINMENT
Attractions and
Counterattractions

"We have to kill time, while waiting for time to kill us."

—Catalan proverb

In some ways, the test of a true Barcelonan is the ability to pass by La Sagrada Familia indifferently, to go week after week without checking the entertainment calendar, and to never look for tickets to major events, with the opera, theater and annual neighborhood festival as possible exceptions. Locals prefer taking to the street or the cafe and hanging out, with niche groups showing up regularly at the entertainment venues that fit their persuasions.

The primary form of entertainment is sharing time with family, friends and neighbors, in parks, bars, outdoor cafes, intimate plazas, and on the beach. On a typical late afternoon or early evening, where it's really happening is at informal public gathering places. But even the most steadfast avoider of night

138

clubs, concerts and other more formalized venues of entertainment will relish taking off on a weekend or summer excursion to enjoy the marvels of Catalonia, whether it be up the coast to the hidden coves of La Costa Brava, north to a Pyrenees ski resort or medieval village, south to the lively beaches of Sitges, or to any one of the monastery retreats, as exemplified by the Benedictine monastery of Montserrat, perched precariously on a rocky mountainside to the east of the city.

THE TEN BEST ATTRACTIONS:
Mainstream and Against the Grain

Even folks who don't like to go out a lot are happy to know that when the urge is upon them, Barcelona can get the job done, with whatever form of entertainment or recreation they want. Let's go out on a limb and choose Barcelona's top ten attractions, each with a non-mainstream alternative. In other cities, this writer is quite happy to skip the mainstream attractions and seek out lesser known features. But Barcelona is such a different city that what it has to offer in the mainstream would be considered countercultural in other places. Gaudi, Miró and the singing poet Joan Manuel Serrat were never conformists.

(1) Gaudi and the Modernists

There won't be much opposition to giving top billing to the buildings and landscape designs of Antoni Gaudi. In the spirit of the medieval times from which it is derived, La Sagrada Familia is taking more than a century to complete, with most sections representing a serious attempt to do what Gaudi would have done had he been alive today. The exception is the work of Josep Subirachs, who is doing it his own way, and probably gets Gaudi's applause from the grave. The 800 pesetas you pay to get in are destined to the finishing of the Gothic-modernist structure, which soars high above the city, in exaltation of faith.

139

The most impressive of the facades is the more detailed one, one of the parts that Gaudi did himself: the Nativity. Climb up through the narrow and twisted passageway and challenge vertigo.

The most playful and mixed-genre Gaudi can be found in Parc Guëll, where everything from stones to colorful mosaics is laid out to fit within an urban forest. Each structure, whether monument, building or asymmetrical stone archway, is different from the next, and joins the natural surroundings with ease. The eye of the observer slides from one curve to another. Gaudi argued that straight lines don't exist in nature, so they shouldn't exist in architecture. One of the structures is Casa Museu Gaudi, with a 300 peseta entry. Parc Guëll is the type of place that deserves a slow-motion visit. On a hot summer day it's a shady spot to get in a day's reading and strolling.

Just when you thought you'd found the last galaxy of Gaudi's universe of imagination, you find Colonia Guëll (Autopista A-2 past Sant Boi de Llobregat or by the Generalitat railroad FGC from Plaça Catalunya). At Colonia Guëll, Gaudi has gone even deeper into being … Gaudi, and seemingly closer to nature, with a larger proportion of sculpted or mosaic stone than in other works of his, and a streamlined lateral movement in the designs.

Other modernist buildings can be seen throughout the city. A walk north from Plaça Catalunya along Passeig de Gràcia brings you past several modernist houses and buildings by Gaudi (1852–1926), Lluis Domènech i Montaner (1849–1923) and Josep Puig i Cadalfalch (1867–1957).

When you reach Plaça de Joan Carles, you'll see more buildings by these three architects and other modernists, to either side along Avinguda Diagonal. Not within this quadrant is one of Domènech i Montaner's most representative buildings, the Palau de la Música (just off Via Laietana, a few hundred meters north of the Cathedral and Gothic Quarter). This architect's structures seem weightier than Gaudi's, with a heavy use of bricks, alternat-

Marta Cañellas

Artistic impression of Gaudí's La Predrera.

Close-up of La Predrera.

ing with colorful patterns of mosaic tiles, sculpted stone and stained glass. The other must-see Domènech i Montaner is the Hopital de Sant Pau (due north from La Sagrada Familia along Passeig de Gaudi). Buildings dedicated to music and health are a reflection of Domènech i Montaner's humanist commitment to civil and public society.

Catalan modernist architecture was partly derived from artistic and historical models of the Middle Ages and has made Barcelona the early twentieth century version of what Florence,

Italy had become since the Renaissance. Much of today's public and aesthetic consciousness among Catalan architects traces back to the modernist period. It would be difficult to label these modernists within the narrow definition of "architect", for they were colorists and sculptors as well.

- **(Alternative 1) The Wonders of Modernist Industrial Architecture**. Here and there in the outlying industrial neighborhoods of Barcelona, as well as the nearby towns, one finds examples of modernist and other daring styles of architecture in factories, many of them abandoned, such as the one along the train tracks just past the town of Montgat, less than 25 kilometers up the coast from the city. Industrial zones like the no-man's land between the seafront and residential neighborhoods of Poblenou contain some of these forgotten works of art. It's more challenging to search for these old modernist factories, for you become an explorer who ventures beyond the obvious. A few of the buildings in Barcelona worth visiting are: Mercat de Sant Antoni (Comte d'Urgell 1 bis), Hydroelectrica de Catalunya (Av. de Vilanova 12), Estació de França (Av. del Marquès at the edge of La Barceloneta), and Escola Industrial (Comte d'Urgell 187). (See: *Rutas del Patrimonio Industrial*, Generalitat de Catalunya, Departament d'Industria, Comerç i Turisme.)

More on industrial architecture in this chapter in the alternative section 10 on excursions. Within the next decade, artists may do a "Soho" with these factories, restoring them into lofts and workshops.

(2) Opera and Concerts in the Gran Teatre del Liceu and Palau de la Música

The Liceu (along Las Ramblas) has now reopened following massive restoration work in the wake of a devastating fire. Remodeling of the Palau de la Música, under the direction of

143

Domènech i Montaner's Palau de la Música.

architect Oscar Tusquets, has achieved a balance between irre-concilable opposites: rigorously respecting the work of Domènech i Montaner and yet adding a concert hall that is up to the standards of modern musical requirements.

Singers of international fame such as Montserrat Caballé and Josep Carreras have continued a profound opera and chorus tradition of Catalonia, with the late Pau Casals as an inspiration for cellists and other classical musicians.

Attend a concert in an unbelievable physical and cultural ambiance.

- **(Alternative 2) The Barcelona Jazz, Salsa and Blues Scene**. Barcelona does not match Paris in its depth of a jazz scene, but don't let that turn you off. One of the twentieth century's great jazz pianists, the blind Tete Monteliu, whom I had the chance to hear in person before he died a few years ago, was a role model for a dynamic generation of up-and-coming musicians, and a young blind pianist by the name of Ignasi Terrasa seems to be continuing where Monteliu left off. During the summer months, keep a lookout for jazz and blues concerts and festivals, many of them free of charge, sponsored by the Escola de Musics and other independent jazz pioneers.

  Many concert bars are eclectic in their offering, so you might find African music at a place that usually programs salsa, or funk and rock at a club known for its jazz. Some of these places have no cover charge while others will ask for up to the equivalent of $10. Pricewise this compares favorably to Paris or New York, as does the price of a beer or mixed drink.

  With late dining hours in Spain, don't expect to hear the first set before 10:30 pm, although I found a few bars on weekday nights where the music began as early as 8:00 pm. A list of the concert bars here would be redundant, since you will need to pick up the *Guía de Ocio* from a newsstand for this and all other types of entertainment. I found some good jazz

Daniel Giordano Leis

Expect to bump into lively jazz festivals in the summer.

combos that were not even listed in the *Guía de Ocio*; poster advertising is yet another traditional art form that survives in Barcelona, and some of the best bets in music will be pasted up on wall or window posters. Several jazz bars are located at or near Plaça Reial, in the Gothic Quarter, a few meters east of Las Ramblas. The eclectic Harlem Jazz Club is as good a place as any to start; you might get jazz, salsa, or a new fashionable genre (Comtessa de Sobradiel, a block south from Plaça de Sant Miguel, phone: 93 310 07 55). Try also Jazz Sí Club (Requesens 2, phone: 93 329 00 20), and La Boite (Av. Diagonal 477, phone: 93 419 59 50).

Our best jazz and blues experiences were found thanks to posted announcements at the neighborhood cafe-bar.

The *cantoautor* (singing poet) music tradition, personified by Lluís Llach and Joan Manuel Serrat, is a homebred performing art that shouldn't be missed. Begin with classic Catalan songs, "Ell S'en Va Content" by Llach and "Quan Arriba el Fred" by Serrat.

(3) The Sardana

The sardana, the most famous Catalan folk dance, has not changed since James Michener's 1968 description: "like the movement of an animated clock that ran in both directions. Slow steps left, slow steps right. Left, right. Left, right, with arms held closely to the side. Then faster steps, with hands slightly raised. Then fast intricate steps, with hands held high above the head and the body swaying beautifully as the tempo of the music increased. Finally the entire plaza in motion ..."

Michener saw the sardana on a Sunday, midday, outside the Cathedral, and today you will still see circles of sardana dancers on a Sunday, midday, outside the Cathedral, accompanied by the somber music of the *cobla* (sardana band) in which, incredibly, one of the primary melody lines is traced by the oboe or *flabiol*.

147

At any given moment, at whichever plaza you await the sardana, it looks as if nothing is going to happen. A woman emerges from among the bystanders, walks to the center, and delicately deposits a handbag on the cobblestones. An older man removes his jacket and places it over the handbag. More jackets and hand-bags are added, and the sardana begins, methodically, with people of all ages, sometimes including children and the elderly, in the same circle.

The sardana comes from the north of Catalonia and seems like the inverse of the flamboyant flamenco from the south of Spain. Flamenco is individualist while sardana is collective. Flamenco is overstatement; sardana, understatement. Flamenco is fire; sardana is embers of Catalan culture that will never be extinguished, a slow but incessant resistance.

Observe the sardana or participate if you can figure out the steps at the Cathedral plaza on Saturdays, 18:30 and Sundays, noon. Plaça Sant Jaume on Sundays at 18:30 gives a Gothic Quar-ter ambiance to the sardana. Winters at noon at the Parc de la Ciutadella or spring through fall at Parc de l'Espanya Industrial are some of the other sardana sites.

- **(Alternative 3) Deeper into Sardana Country**. Sunday in small-town Catalonia. One of our fondest memories was a walk up from the coast just north of Barcelona to the town of Alella, where we intended to observe the sardana. Our son was only four years old at the time and had not yet acquired any of the self-consciousness that comes with maturity. As we sat on the bench with other people from the nearby villages, our son jumped into the circle and was welcomed by two young women who took his hands and guided him through the movements.

  In Barcelona, the sardana unfolds in the midst of commotion. People come out of cathedrals, pass by on their way to art galleries or sporting events, or hurry to meet their friends. Buses glide by, marchers protesting privatization of public enterprises,

Sardana dancers.

149

panhandlers, would-be pickpockets, kids with soccer balls on the way to the park.

In small towns not far from the city, the sardana gets undivided attention. The whole community gathers around the dancers, and even if you sit on a bench and watch, you are part of the spectacle. The sardana becomes the focal point of a community gathering, the expression, without demagoguery, of solidarity. It is like the hymn of a nation in the form of a complex dance with surprisingly somber music. The subtle and mellow joy of the sardana is something best experienced in a setting where external distractions are totally absent, as the village plaza seems to hover above time, floating through the nebulous images of Catalonia's past generations.

(4) Barça Football

In 1899, the year after Spain lost its last American colonies, the Barcelona football ("soccer" to Americans) club was founded. Throughout its history, it has transcended the athletic field and become a symbol of Catalonia's struggle for autonomy and freedom from Spanish dictatorships like those of Primo de Rivera and Franco. Like the New York Yankees in American baseball or Manchester United in England, FC Barcelona has been the dominant football team in its league. Matches against Real de Madrid are legendary, as are European Cup games.

A 475 peseta entry into the Museu del Futbol Club Barcelona includes a visit to the stadium at Camp Nou (Metro Collblanc, phone: 93 496 36 00 for museum or tickets). Tickets for games are available at the stadium or through banks. The cheapest tickets are 3,000 pesetas, about US$20. If attending a Barça game is an occasional luxury, skip the cheapest seats and go for something closer to the action. Otherwise, bring a good pair of binoculars.

The team's slogan is "More than a Club", and to support Barça is considered an act of faith in Catalonia. There are 104,000 club members (for a stadium with 110,000 seats), and from its

Rafa Segui

Barça football: an unbeatable spectacle.

past political resistance, the club has become a financial mover and shaker.

- **(Alternative 4) Club Espanyol football**. Many of the players on Barça's team are glamorous foreigners, with Rivaldo from Brazil as the star of the millennium. Few if any players are from Catalonia. The real team of Barcelona (although only a few iconoclasts will agree with this) is Reial Club Deportiu Espanyol. Espanyol usually fields a significant contingent of hometown players. They rarely finish in the top half of the standings, but at least their on-field presence is Catalan.

  Espanyol, founded one year after Barça, plays its home games in the more cozy Estadi Olímpic in Montjuïc. For tickets, phone 93 424 88 00.

151

(5) Art Museums

Pablo Picasso and Joan Miró head the list of great Catalan paint-ers. The Picasso Museum and Miró Foundation get top billing for any mainstream art tour. Visiting these two museums in the same day offers a dramatic contrast. The Picasso Museum is housed in a stone medieval structure on Montcada 15-19, near the urban center of town, while the Miró Foundation, in the wooded Parc de Montjuïc, is an impressive example of avant-garde architecture built by the daring architect Josep Lluis Sert.

Picasso spent a large part of his life in France, in exile from the Franco dictatorship, but he never lost his love for his Catalan homeland, and in 1962 agreed to donate a large collection of his work for the Picasso Museum. Those of us who depart from Picasso exhibits disappointed at not finding enough from his earlier realist periods, will be pleasantly rewarded here. The "blue period" and other earlier styles are well represented, with enough from all his periods, and including other media such as ceramics and engravings, to please the most picky Picasso fanatic. Entrance: 600 pesetas, 250 pesetas on Wednesdays, and free the first Sunday of each month.

The Miró Foundation has the world's best collection of this playful artist's work: nearly 300 paintings, 150 sculptures, textiles, engravings, and 7,000 drawings. Before visiting, check it out at www.bcn.fjmiro.es or call 34 93 329 19 08. Entry: 700 pesetas. Both Picasso and Miró began with their own styles of realism. Picasso became a cubist while Miró created a unique form of sur-realism, more abstract than figurative. An interesting contrastive tour would be to watch the somber sardanas with their understated and hidden joy in front of the Cathedral at midday on Sunday and then head over to the Miró Foundation to take in the sur-realist's gregarious, primary colors. Such a contrast will convince those in search of simple cultural stereotypes that Catalonia's multiple and contradictory dimensions are too complex for simplistic analysis.

For broader and chronological views of Catalan art, try the Museu d'Art Modern (MNAC), Parc de la Ciutadella, Plaça d'Armes (93 319 57 28, 500 pts) and the Museu d'Art Contemporani de Barcelona (MACBA), Plaça dels Angels (93 412 08 10, 600 pts), in that order.

- **(Alternative 5) With Independent Galleries**, the astonishment index rises, for you have no preconceived notion of what to expect. Especially throughout the Gothic Quarter, the stroller will bump into these boutique-style galleries. Entrance is free, and you need not have your checkbook ready. Villa del Arte (Arcs 5, less than 100 meters from the Cathedral) is one of them, displaying a collection of very different artists, both Catalan and foreign, so you're bound to find a style that keeps you entranced. Once you pick out what you like, the artist will likely be on hand for questions or comments, something not possible with Picasso and Miró.

There I saw "Cafe et d'épée," an eerie anachronistic street scene by Dutch painter Nemo Jantzen, which for me better interpreted the Gothic Quarter atmosphere than any of the postcards that overflow from nearby boutiques.

Dalí. When astonishment is the theme in the realm of art, Salvador Dalí's name inevitably pops up. In the international art world Dalí may have preferred to be known as a Spaniard rather than a Catalan, but he was born and died in the Catalan city of Figueres, only a couple of hours by train from Plaça Catalunya. Dalí was not only an artist with agile technical skills and a penchant for surrealism (more surrealist than the movement's leaders who rejected him in 1934), but he was, above all, a magical entertainer. His magic came from the dazzling techniques of his paintbrush, and his calculated eccentricity. Were it not for this impeccable technical mastery in his works, one might take him for a P.T. Barnum, although it is doubtful he expected to be taken seriously when he claimed,

Painting and photo by Nemo Jantzen

Imagine yourself waking up from a time machine in a medieval alley in Barcelona.

for example, that he could remember what it was like when he was in his mother's womb.

Given Dalí's extravagant showmanship, be expected to be truly entertained at his Teatre-Museu Dalí in Figueres, where the painter himself was buried. Outside the old municipal theater where the museum is housed is a one-of-a-kind sculpture display, strange, dreamlike figures against the facade and in the museum's front plaza. Within, don't expect a typical gallery. Every wall, floor, table, ceiling and window is calculated with an artistic hand to dazzle the visitor, with paintings, sculptures, and many undefined genres, guaranteed to please the most diehard museum haters. Many of his paintings (and objects arranged to form three-dimension "paintings") are double exposures with two completely different representations, whose relationship may be totally absurd. A blink of the eyes helps switch from one exposure to the other. There are paintings on metal tubes whose reflections upon tabletops where they stand portray a totally different image. Example: a painting of flowers on a vertical tube, whose reflection on the table is a portrait of Don Quixote and Sancho Panza. Entrance: 1,000 pts, with that price lowered in the off-season and hiked on prime-time summer evenings. (Information: 972 50 31 55)

(6) Amusement Parks

Barcelona has two great amusement parks, both in panoramic contexts. The Parque de Atracciones, on Montjuïc, is surrounded by gardens, with a superb view of the city and port. There are 40 different rides and an open-air theater with summer concerts. Entrance: 700 pts, with special group rates and free for children under three, phone: 93 441 70 24. Metro Paral.lel, Lines 2 or 3, plus buses 61 or 101. At this writing, the park is closed, awaiting a decision to reopen or shut down.

Even more spectacular is the Parc d'Atraccions Tibidabo, 500 meters above sea level in the Collserola Mountains outside

155

Barcelona, also with a panoramic view of the city and port, featuring a terrorific theater spectacle. The most picturesque way to get here is by the Tramvia Blau, which leaves you at the foot of the funicular for the last leg of the journey. There's also a Tibibus leaving Plaça Catalunya, which runs more or less frequently depending on the season, and a train from Plaça Catalunya. The park is open from Holy Week through October. Entrance: 1,000 pts (rides and spectacles not included), with special school and group rates. A Tibidabo "Pasaporte" gives you unlimited rides during a particular season for 7,000 pts. Phone: 93 211 79 42. Also check out the Temple del Sagrat Cor (Sacred Heart), with a giant Christ, and an elevator that takes you to the top for an exceptional view; or the Collserola Tower, 280 meters above, with a glass elevator taking you more than 100 meters up for a view that, on a clear day, extends out for 60 kilometers.

- **(Alternative 6) Diffusement Parks**. Some people find nothing amusing about amusement parks, and are looking for a real park, one where waiting in line for brief thrills is replaced by extended pleasure in a naturally sensorial setting. Barcelonans who visit Tibidabo once every two or three years might visit Parc de la Ciutadella several times each month, and still they discover nooks and crannies where one can find a bit of herby solitude. Meditators can make brief forays from their point of refuge to a museum (modern art), a world-famous zoo (with shade trees and benches for the slow motion visitor), a waterfall gushing out through an avant-garde landscape design of molded stone, and the picturesque rowboats. The modernist "Arc de Triomf" is the gateway to the park, in an arabesque design with detailed brickwork by architect Josep Vilaseca.

    Montjuïc, for its panoramic views and walking paths, and Parc Guëll, for its playful Gaudi ambiance, are other favorites of park goers. Montjuïc combines amusement and diffusement, including the world's first and most authentic theme park, Poble

Espanyol, and a park within a park in Parc Joan Miró, with a huge woman-and-bird sculpture by Miró. Theme park haters are challenged to give it one last chance at Poble Espanyol, with truly impressive renditions of building styles from throughout Spain, from medieval to Moorish, and Andalusian, Basque and other Spanish street scenes. Entrance to Poble Espanyol is a thousand pesetas, but except for prime-time nights on Friday and Saturday, there's free admission after 9:00 pm. During the summer it's still light at that hour, and Poble Espanyol has its attractive nightlife.

With such seductive parks, one of the best for pure nature is sometimes overlooked. Parc de Palau Reial (Metro Palau Reial) may occupy fewer acres than its more well-known counterparts, but within, nature is at its most intense, and you'll always be able to set aside your own solitary plot of shady terrain. Behind the park, a former royal residence contains a ceramics museum, a decorative arts museum, and beyond that, a Gaudí house.

(7) Beaches

Beginning at La Barceloneta and moving up the coast in a northerly direction, and in and around Sitges to the south, are the splendid beaches of the Barcelona region. (Inveterate iconoclasts preferred these beaches in their seedier pre-Olympic days.) An attractive post-Olympic boardwalk stretches along the northerly coast from the city. Cyclists, rollerbladers, food stands specializing in fish, and a few shopping centers add to the already appealing beach scene, and the beach at the Olympic Village offers a variety of nautical sports.

Even though Dave and Kathy Smoley are ocean lovers, it took them a while to become adjusted to Barcelona beaches, given the topless women sunbathers. Kathy says she felt like a prude wearing her top. But after their initial shock, their three kids became indifferent to the spectacle. Toplessness at some beaches

is attributed to French and German tourists, but on one of our favorite beaches at El Masnou, even during the month before the inflow of tourists, the locals had already set the topless standard. At times one observed three generations of topless women: grandma, mother and daughter.

"Wearing my top," said my wife, "made me feel like an exhibitionist."

But time heals these culture shocks, and in the end, the beach is the beach. When choosing a spot for settling down, try to keep away from rivers or rivulets that flow down from the mountains. Barcelona tourism authorities won't broadcast this news, but especially after storms, these channels may carry raw wastes directly into the sea.

Tossa de Mar. For true bathing elegance, take a train to Blanes and connecting bus to the first town on the northern Costa Brava that has not been ruined by high-rise ugliness. Tossa de Mar, Marc Chagall's "blue paradise", has emerald waters, hidden rocky coves, ruins of a Roman villa on a nearby hill, and a well-preserved cobblestone town. We've done the trip twice and got there early enough to have a whole day and return in the evening to Barcelona. But Tossa is worth an overnight stay. A quicker round trip from Barcelona, less than an hour and a half, is with SARFA buses (phone: 972 30 06 23), for less than a thousand pesetas round trip.

- **(Alternative 7)** Here are a few choices according to your persuasions. If you're not too rebellious but like getting away from the hordes, the **Costa Brava north of Tossa** is worth the trip. At least one overnight stay is necessary, more preferred. You're now in the territory of the great Catalan prose stylist and travel writer Josep Pla. Every beach and village along the way has its own unique charm, whether it be Roman ruins, rocky coves with hidden beaches, or friendly villages. Calella de Palafrugell is a fine central base, and the home of an annual *Habaneras* concert the first Saturday in July, along with some influence of Catalans who had traveled to Cuba during the colonial period. A bus from Barcelona will get you there in two hours for between US$10 and $15. Phone: SARFA (972 30 06 23). Hotels, campgrounds, kayaking, hiking, fishing, and aquatic parks are just a few of the attractions. The Patronat Municipal de Tourisme in Blanes will send you free information on hotels. Fax: 34 972 33 46 86. If you like friendly, family-run hotels, consider Hotel Sant Roc, phone: 972 61 42 50.

  The northernmost region, L'Alt Emporda, is the most rugged, with the whitewashed town of Cadaqués as its central location. Nearby you'll find Port Lligat, the favorite second-home hangout of Salvador Dalí. The central El Baix Emporada is the most exquisite, with unbelievable towering rock formations decorating the beaches. If you have the time, trips from here to the Pyrenees Mountains and the medieval city of Girona will help complete the perfect vacation.

  Other more alternative beaches are found at the seaside city of Sitges, known for its nightlife. Distinct beaches are separated by dikes, with a boardwalk connecting them all. Among these specialty beaches are a heterosexual nudist beach and a gay nudist beach.

  The beaches along Le Maresme, halfway between Barcelona and La Costa Brava, minimize the effects of tourism with a traditional, local cultural scenario.

(8) Bullfights

In the realm of spectator events, bullfights pale in popularity among Barcelonans in comparison to football. Official tourist publications mention bullfighting in passing; they have to recognize it's there, but too much applause and they'd come out looking like apologists for what many foreigners see as cruelty to animals. Defenders of bullfighting trot out a litany of arguments: the "hypocrisy" of meat eaters, who while never having witnessed the slow slaughter of a pig, dismiss bullfighting as an act of cruelty; or of those who, while condemning the violence of bullfighting, accept the glorification of violence in movies and on TV, or condone the death penalty knowing statistically that a certain number of innocent people will be among the electrocuted.

Among the small subculture of bullfighting fanatics are those who, becoming spokesmen for the bull, tell us that the bull would rather die in combat than in a slaughterhouse. Many of them argue that bullfighting is an art, depending on the grace and wit of the bullfighter, a type of courageous dance at the edge of death.

Aside from the unhappy bull, the unfortunate horses that carry the *picadores* to prod the bull are the victims of the bull's bloody attacks of self-defense, even though they're blindfolded and protected by padding. The horses are the forgotten victims of the spectacle. I am still waiting to hear a debate between a bull-fighting enthusiast and a horse lover who opposes the death penalty and TV violence.

Two *banderilleros* enter to implant colorful darts in the bull's gorge. The dramatic moment arrives when the bullfighter matches wits with his respected but mortal enemy. It is not a question of when he kills the bull but with what degree of artistry he does it, and only after he's given the bull ample opportunity to defend itself. Audience participation has something to do with the result, for the bullfighter must make his passes with excellence and agility in order to receive the shouts of approval that allow him to cut off the bull's ear.

A significant number of Barcelonans go through their whole life without ever attending a bullfight. If you still want to go, you'll enter a magnificently designed Plaça de Toros Monumental, Gran Via Corts Catalanes, at the "Monumental" metro stop. The season runs from early April to the end of September, with the spectacle beginning on Sundays between 17:00 and 18:00. Tickets are between 2,100 and 12,000 pts, ticket windows are on Muntaner 24, and the phone is 93 453 69 98.

- **(Alternative 8) Flamenco: the Bullfights without the Bull**. The costume of a bullfighter might as well be that of a flamenco dancer. For the uninitiated, the movements of the *torero* and the flamenco dancer are not far apart. One of Barcelona's flamenco clubs is actually named after the great bullfighter, El Cordobés. Like *los toros, el flamenco* is not native to the Catalonia region, and you have to go out of your way to find it. It's a sensual dance from Andalusia in the south of Spain. Check the musicology department of the local library for the various theories on how flamenco music and dance developed from a blend of Moorish, Gypsy, Flemish and Latin influences.

161

Flamenco is not a Catalan genre but you will find it in Barcelona. I actually bumped into flamenco music when visiting a "social center" that squatters had set up in an abandoned building. Although a minority, immigrants from southern Spain make up an important sector of the Barcelona population, and flamenco is one element from their culture.

Flamenco clubs include: Al-Andalus, Moianes 16 (phone: 93 331 06 54); Los Almonleños, Elkano 67 (93 443 24 31); Cordobés, La Rambla 35 (93 317 57 11); Macarena, Llanca 5 (93 209 38 06); El Patio Andaluz, Aribau 242 (93 209 35 24); Tablao de Carmen, at Poble Espanyol in Montjuïc (93 325 68 95); and Los Tarantos, Plaça Reial 17 (93 318 30 67). Be prepared to fork out from 3,500 pts for a show and two drinks to as much as 8,500 pts for entrance with dinner plus the spectacle.

(9) Cinema

With so much going on, who needs to go to the movies in a place like Barcelona? First of all, for film fanatics, there's a Filmoteca de la Generalitat de Catalunya, including not only high quality cinema but a specialized library: Cine Aquitania, Av. Sarria 33 (phone: 93 410 75 90). Another exceptional cinema experience is the elegant Imax Port Vell, one of the world's few floating cinemas, just across from the Maremagnum shopping center. For between 850 pts on workday mornings and 1,500 pts at night, you can witness the Omnimax, movies projected on a spherical screen 180 degrees around, or a 3D salon if you wish.

Another important reason you may wish to attend the movies in Catalonia is to view a film in English with Catalan subtitles, or one you've already seen in English with Catalan dubbing. A new law mandates that a certain percentage of foreign movies must have Catalan translations. For the learner of Catalan, attending the cinema becomes an educational experience, provided that the learner chooses familiar themes to bridge the language gap.

- **(Alternative 9) The Theater Scene**. Many theater presentations are in Catalan, some in Spanish, and very few in English, so a language barrier must be considered. There are at least 26 regular theaters, and smaller theater groups may be found at unlisted venues. A list of the theaters here would not compare with the *Guía del Ocio*, absolutely necessary in order to know in advance the language of the presentation, its theme, cost of tickets and curtain times. Language learners attending the theater should be aware that when one is not involved in a dialogue, the eavesdropping mode takes over and it's more difficult to understand what's going on.

   That said, some theaters may be presenting dramas or comedies you've already seen in your own language, thereby providing a familiar context for your language learning. Some of the smaller theaters have an offbeat, off-off-Broadway ambiance. Such theaters offer the chance to get to know what's being done by local playwrights. When music is part of the presentation, you'll have that international language to facilitate comprehension. Advanced tickets are available through Caixa Catalunya (phone: 902 10 12 12). Tiquet-3 is a system in which tickets are sold at the office of Barcelona Tourism, Plaça de Catalunya, within three hours of the performance.

(10) Excursions

Expect lively breakfast table discussions on which excursion site to choose from; the menu seems infinite. If we follow the crowd, we can establish a certain order of preference. Remarkably, both tourists and local residents often like to visit the same places, so the alienation of visiting a place in a new country only to find all foreigners there is unlikely to repeat itself in the Barcelona region. On the top of the mainstream list is the magnificent Costa Brava, up the coast in the direction of the French border. We've already referred to the emerald coves, Roman ruins, and other features of the Costa Brava under "Beaches", the unconventional Sitges, also

163

Manuel Iglesias

Adventurous builders of the Middle Ages chose out-of-the-way places like Montserrat, but invaders sacked the place; it was rebuilt in the nineteenth century.

under "Beaches" and the Dalí museum ("Art Museums"). Those three top the list for excursions outside Barcelona.

Montserrat. Another "must" visit if you agree with the crowd is Montserrat, in the Sawtooth Mountains 50 kilometers northwest of Barcelona. The engineering feats of the Benedictine monks in building their eleventh century monastery on a mountain ledge more than 700 meters above sea level is enough reason to honor this place with a visit. Some come here to gawk while others are serious pilgrims with a mission. The spectacular ascension via *teleférico* cablecar above the Llobregat valley from the train station to the monastery is unforgettable. Choose a clear day and you'll see the Pyrenees Mountains at the French border, and maybe even a few islands in the Mediterranean.

The monastery was conquered and sacked by Napoleon's troops at the beginning of the nineteenth century, to be abandoned until its reconstruction began in 1858, so the original architecture of other Benedictine monasteries in Catalonia is more intact. But Montserrat's geographic setting and spiritual significance make it worth the trip. Nearly a hundred monks live here, welcoming pilgrims who have come to see the Black Virgin, *La Morenata*, the patron saint of Catalonia. Within the complex is a museum with everything from Egyptian and Gothic relics to contemporary art, a sixteenth century basilica, and a children's chorus. To look down upon the monastery, take a tram to 250 meters above, although a 3 kilometer trek to the same spot is more in keeping with the pilgrim theme of the site. For overnight stays in campsites, shared hostel rooms or a hotel, phone 93 835 02 01. You can get to Montserrat in a Julia Tours bus from the Sants bus station (round trip approximately 1,300 pts, more or less depending on the time and day) or by the train-funicular-teleférico combination, departing from Plaça Espanya, with several price formulas, the most expensive, including cable car and tram: 2,530, adults, about half that for children.

Girona. Medieval lovers will be thrilled by a trip to Girona, which can be done in conjunction with a stay on the Costa Brava, 35 kilometers away, or in combination with a visit to the Dalí theater-museum in Figueres, the next city up the road north of Girona. El Call was a large Middle Ages Jewish community. Here the Centre Bonastruc Ça Porta provides expositions on what Jewish life was like in medieval times. Girona's multicultural theme continues with a visit to the Banys Arabs, which the Moors had built in the Roman style to serve the Christians, some three centuries before Spain coalesced into a nation. Other medieval treats in Girona include the houses along the river Onyar from the end of the Middle Ages, the baroque Gothic cathedral and twelfth century Roman cloisters, and other churches and convents in the old quarter within the remaining sections of its medieval rampart. Entrance into Girona's museums is less expensive than their Barcelona counterparts.

Girona's Romanesque and Gothic medieval setting is complemented by Roman and Renaissance styles. Tip! Most visitors to Girona are not aware of the old factory, Farinera Teixidor (Santa Eugenia 42), a 1911 construction by the architect Rafael Masó, with a bizarre stylistic mix of the d'Hoffmann Vienna school and Gaudi's modernism, combining iron, stone and ceramic building materials.

Trains for Girona depart from Plaça Catalunya and other Barcelona stations. In Girona, visit the Oficina de Turismo, Rambla de la Llibertat 1, or call 972 22 65 75.

Cava Tour. *Cava* is the Catalan and Spanish version of bubbly champagne. Cava- and wine-tasting tours are centered in the l'Alt Penedés region, only 40 kilometers south of Barcelona, primarily in and around the towns of Sant Sadurni d'Anoia and the larger Vilafranca del Penedés. Choosing between the more than 300 wine and cava producers in the region is a daunting task, and the best strategy is to seek multilingual advice from the Oficina de Turismo de Vilafranca del Penedés, Cort 14 (phone: 93 892 03 58, website: www.ajvilafranca.es).

The leading Spanish producer of *cava* is the Raventós family, whose property, Can Codorniu, dates back to the sixteenth century. Their 26 kilometers of stone arched wine cellars were built by none other than the great modernist architect, Puig i Cadalfalch, between 1896 and 1906. To get around the cellar you need to take a mini-train. This might be a good place to begin the wine-champagne tour.

RENFE trains arrive here from Arc de Triomf, Plaça Catalunya and Sants stations. For the bus option, call Hispano Igualdina, 93 430 43 44. It may be more strategic to rent a car, if you plan on hopping to as many wineries as possible.

Tarragona. Fans of Roman culture will place Tarragona on the top of their excursion list. Today a modern city of 110,000 inhabitants, Tarragona was founded as Tarraco by the Romans in 218 and 205 B.C., on high land overlooking the Mediterranean. Beginning in the Middle Ages, it was a seat of an important archdiocese. Today it is an important commercial port. Palisades overlooking the Mediterranean, numerous archeological ruins, and a cathedral with both Gothic and Romanesque styles built between the twelfth and fourteenth centuries are impressive landmarks of Tarragona.

Within the city itself, driving from west to east parallel to the coast, the visitor can see: an early Christian burial ground, with beautifully carved sarcophagi; a colonial forum; the amphi-theater, overlooking the sea; a Roman circus originally used for chariot races (81-96 A.D.); the Torre dels Escipions, a funeral monument with high reliefs; an archeological museum; a provincial forum; and a stretch of the ancient ramparts and their majestic towers, with portals leading to the Passeig Arqueologic, a prom-enade between the walls and eighteenth century fortifications. Three kilometers north of the city is a towering aqueduct, the Pont de les Ferreres, also known as the "Bridge of the Devil", made of reddish gold-colored stone, probably dating back to the first century A.D. during the reign of Augustus.

Ask for information at the Patronato de Turismo, Major 39, or call 977 24 52 03.

- **(Alternative 10) Exploring Catalonia**. Alternative-minded travelers find it difficult to maintain an iconoclast stance in the realm of Barcelona excursions, since all the above mainstream trips will satisfy the most demanding alternative tastes. You can go to Paris and, with no regrets, not visit EuroDisneyland, and you can have an enriching stay in New York without going to the top of the World Trade Center; but you can't go to Barcelona without visiting the quirky Dalí theater-museum or La Costa Brava.

  Nevertheless, once you've gotten to Catalonia's main excursion sites, you'll remain with a perplexing menu of exciting and adventurous itineraries. The Costa Brava itself hides many lesser-known coves of rugged beauty, with Roman ruins overlooking the sea. Deep within the mountains of Catalonia, well-preserved medieval villages with Romanesque and Gothic structures await the most intrepid travelers. Hiking, climbing and skiing in the rugged Pyrenees Mountains is a worthy test for most audacious adventurers.

168

The Generalitat of Catalonia, Department of Industry, Commerce and Tourism, has prepared thematic itineraries, based on ancient past, Renaissance and baroque art, Romanesque art, and Industrial Patrimony. Many of these routes overlap, and anyone with limited travel time would do best to combine all four categories into one. A fifth category will also overlap: adventuring in the Pyrenees.

Hiking. Both the Costa Brava and Pyrenees regions have numerous footpaths. Check in at the local tourism office of your point of departure for maps and information. You may be told that trails will be marked. Having done a fair amount of hiking in Europe, I can advise that caution must be exercised. At times, trail marks are missing, especially in and out of towns. The absolute rule is to stay on the trail. You don't want to be astray during hunting season.

History addicts may wish to trace the paths of international brigades as they entered Spain over the Pyrenees to fight in the civil war, which for many became the same paths of escape a year or two later. The rugged charm of the Pyrenees is still intact: primitive villages, deep gorges, unexpected geographic quirks.

One example of a Catalonia hike: the *Ruta del Carrilet*, approximately 40 kilometers (25 miles) from Girona (described above) to Olot, over the path once occupied by an old railroad line. When you arrive in Olot, in the center of a volcanic zone officially declared a natural park, you will find several examples of superb industrial architecture: *La Fábrica Descals*, Vilanova Street, built in 1917 by architect Joan Roca i Pinet and *La Fábrica Bassols*, Av. Girona 2, built by the same architect in 1916. Also in Olot are many examples of baroque and Renaissance art, including the El Carme Monastery, founded in 1565, and several chapels with baroque altarpieces. The Garrotxa regional museum, volcanic zone natural park, and

169

the impressive reddish-stone monastery, Sant Joan les Fonts, add to Olot's attractions.

While in Olot, ask the people to point you to the El Greco painting, "Christ Carrying the Cross", one of the most powerful works by El Greco, hanging in the parish church of Sant Esteve, a fitting end to a pilgrimage.

When well planned, your hikes will begin and end at sites of cultural interest with lodging facilities. (Consult the Oficina de Turismo in Girona: 972 22 65 75.)

Skiing. Spain's first ski resorts, now updated with the most modern equipment, are found in the Girona Pyrenees, at Guils Fontanera, Masella, La Molina, Vall de Núria, and Vallter. Here are the longest ski runs in the Catalan Pyrenees, with spectacular scenery. These and the Andorra resorts farther northwest offer the best skiing and boarding value in Europe.

Most folks travel from Barcelona to go duty-free shopping in Andorra. The tiny principality of 65,000 inhabitants survives on commerce. What Andorra may lack in the "daylong downhill glides" of Alps ski resorts is compensated for by its accessibility (no long hours on treacherous roads to get there) and price (lift tickets are only about US$25 in high season and less if you get a multi-day ticket). Andorra's two largest resorts are the Soldeu-el Tartar complex (www.soldeu.ad.) and Pas de la Casa-Grau Roig complex (www.pasgrau.com), only a half hour drive from the capital, Andorra la Vella. Lift tickets at the smaller resort, Arinsal/Pal (www.arinsal.ad.) are US$17.

Andorra might be one of the smallest countries in the world. Attempts to field a "duty-free" soccer team in international competition have met with disastrous results. The dominant language of Andorra is Catalan.

Village Hopping. One day I'd love to do a book on the Catalonia equivalent to Reader's Digest's *100 Most Beautiful*

Villages in France. Many of the most unusual villages are off the bus and train routes, so an automobile becomes the best means of transportation, unless you're a cross-country trekker. Here are a few places that win nominations for the list of villages.

Abella de la Conca, reached by dirt road (nearest city, Tremp; northwest of Barcelona at the foot of the Pyrenees), looks like a third-world village, perched at the edge of a gorge with vertical mountains in the background. Unexpectedly, you find the former parish church of Sant Esteve d'A, Romanesque, with Lombard decoration, and a two-story bell tower.

Besalú, in the La Garrotxa region, northwest of Girona, is living testimony of medieval and post-Middle Ages coexistence between Catholics and the Jewish community: churches of Sant Pere, Sant Vincenç, Santa Maria and Sant Martí, and the *miqwé* Jewish baths. You'll be wondering "Who needs the twenty-first century?" when you contemplate Besalú's twelfth century bridge. For an overnight stay, consider Fonda Siques "Cal Parent", for about US$30 including all meals, and with a swimming pool.

Cardona (north of Manresa; west of Barcelona) has one of the great Catalan Romanesque monuments, the former Sant Vincenç de C basilica from the year 1040, built in the shape of a cross on a hilltop overlooking a green valley.

Castellfollit de la Roca and other villages of the Oix make up an area in La Garrotxa for those who yearn for primitive nature: thick mountains with stunning rock formations and deep gorges, amidst wild green native vegetation, and the ruins of an ancient medieval castle, Castellfollit de la Roca, with spectacular basalt walls.

Castellnou d'Ossó is an unassuming farming village in Urgell (west of Barcelona; closest city, Lleida) whose claim to fame is the preserved remains of an important Roman fortification. The foundation is in the shape of an irregular semicircle, 30

Manuel Iglesias

Two views of the twelfth century bridge in Besalú.

meters long and 4 meters high. The structure has a double wall. A few houses adjoin the structure. During the medieval period, the structure was used by farmers. They filled it with soil to raise the level of the ground. A circular tower was built inside.

La Seu d'Urgell (northern Catalonia, just south of Andorra) is a city with an antiquity-lovers' twelfth century cathedral, Santa Maria, the most impressive examples of Italian-style Romanesque architecture in Catalonia. This city makes the list here because of its strategic location, within striking distance of numerous smaller and quainter medieval villages.

Puigcerda makes this list for sentimental reasons. It's a border town, right across from the living-relic town of La Tour de Carol in France. The town itself is not impressive, but the 1922 railroad station with its pointed roofs and striking masonry is worth the long stay you'll probably be subjected to as you wait for the next train. The setting is in the green Segre Valley in the heart of the Pyrenees, which has made a lasting impression on this observer.

Rupit, 85 kilometers northeast from Barcelona, is one of the most ancient and best-preserved villages in all of Catalonia, built on a slab of stone that still serves as its pavement. Houses are of stone facades with overhanging wood balconies, and heavy carved-wood doors.

Sant Pere de Rodes (northern section of the Costa Brava; nearest city, Roses) is the alternative Montserrat: another Benedictine monastery in a pre-Romanesque style, with fewer modern alterations than its Montserrat counterpart, and offering a spectacular view overlooking the sea and coastal villages. Traces of fresco paintings have been found in a lower cloister. It was declared a World Heritage Site by UNESCO. A jump down to the town of Roses and you'll find a citadel, founded by the ancient Greeks in the fifth century, with Roman, medieval and Renaissance additions.

Manuel Iglesias

Manuel and his daughter enjoy a stone-slab street in Rupit.

Santa Pau, southeast of Olot, is built around a medieval castle, with overlapping stone arcades of different dimensions, hidden in a volcanic mountain zone.

Terrassa's three Visigothic-Romanesque churches dating back to the sixth and seventh centuries make this a worthy stop, with twelfth century alterations in Lombard style. This is a short excursion north from Barcelona through Sant Cugat del Valles, whose fully restored former Benedictine monastery (twelfth century) is a must stopover.

These are but a few nominations for the potential village hopper in Catalonia. The village of Besalú, strategically located between the Costa Brava and the Pyrenees, might be the best aesthetic focal point for access to some of the villages mentioned here, and many others worthy of inclusion. Village hoppers will inevitably drive through cities and towns scarred by utilitarian Franco-era apartment buildings and be tempted to step on the gas and continue onward, until an exciting baroque detail catches the eye: the wood-carved doorway of a church, an ancient Roman bridge, a first-millennium house ... images that are worthy of extended contemplation. The farther off the main route, the greater probability of discovering the most perfectly preserved grainy ensembles of Catalan medieval heritage.

P.S. Last Tips on Barcelona Attractions

Most museums are closed on Mondays. For between 2,500 and 3,500 pesetas you can purchase a "Barcelona Card", allowing you free public transportation and offering discounts of 30–50 percent, but the Barcelona Card is designed only for guerrilla visitors who descend upon the city for one-to-three-day incursions and then withdraw. Phone: 902 10 12 12; in-person at Turisme de Barcelona offices at Plaça de Catalunya 17-S, Plaça de Sant Jaume, and the Sants train station.

For a single fee of 1,700 pesetas for a day and 2,300 for two days, the tourist has unlimited trips on the Bus Turistic, which passes by all the major tourist sites.

Long-term visitors have it better, if they set aside the first Saturday or Sunday of the month for free museum going. A number of museums offer free entry late afternoons. Various small specialty museums are free to the public at all times.

Tickets for many events are on sale wherever it says *Servi-Caixa* (phone: 902 33 22 11).

175

Museums Free of Charge the First Sunday (or Saturday) of Each Month

Museu Barbier-Mueller, pre-Columbian Art, Montcada 14 (phone: 93 319 76 03). Saturday.

Museu Etnologic, Passeig de Santa Madrona, Parc Montjuïc (phone: 93 424 64 02). Sunday.

Museu de las Arts Decoratives, Palau de Pedralbes, Av. Diagonal 686 (phone: 93 280 50 24). Sunday.

Museu Frederic Mares, Gothic Quarter, Carrer dels Comtes, medieval sculpture, items from daily life in ancient times (phone: 93 310 58 00). Sunday.

Museu-Monastir de Pedralbes, fourteenth century, Gothic, frescos, Baixada Monestir 9 (phone: 93 203 92 82). Sunday.

Museu Textil i d'Indumentari, Moncada 12 (phone: 93 310 45 16). Saturday.

Museus de Geologia and Zoologia, Parc de la Ciutadella (phone: 93 319 68 95 and 93 319 69 50 respectively). Sunday.

Museu d'Historia de la Ciutat, Plaça del Rei, including underground Roman ruins (phone: 93 315 11 11). Wednesday.

Museu de la Música, Av. Diagonal 373 (phone: 93 416 11 57). Sunday.

Museu Picasso, Montcada 15-19 (phone: 93 319 63 10). Sunday.

Chapter Ten

CALENDAR
The Year of Living Excessively

"When the cold days are over
the people awaken."

(Quan s'acaba el fred
desperten els homes.)

—from a song by Joan Manuel Serrat

Newcomers to Barcelona can be overwhelmed by the extraordinary number of annual events, both festivals and fairs. The festival calendar is probably more replete in warmer southern Spain, but it never gets cold enough in Barcelona to dim the festival spirit, and the newcomer must solve the festival calendar puzzle, picking and choosing which events to attend.

Should you go all out and participate in as many annual events as possible, complementing the hard work of the year with hard partying? Or, like some neighbors do, should you leave town just before the festival arrives? For time-sensitive individuals, there are two schools of thought. The first option, showing up at all the events, assumes that by filling one's life with peak and spiritually replenishing moments, psychological time expands and life seems longer. The opposing point of view argues that the time leading up to these great moments is wasted on anticipation, while post-festival recovery periods adds so much more filler. Such a significant amount of time congealing around single events numerically reduces the year's milestones, making one feel that life passes by more quickly.

When planning a long stay in a festival city like Barcelona, deciding how to deal with annual events is nearly as important as choosing an apartment or seeking a job. Yet, this issue goes unaddressed in most travel books. Barcelona residents deal with the annual event scenario in two opposite ways, as illustrated with a typical example: the Festa Major de Gràcia/Fiesta Mayor de Gràcia in August. (This is Barcelona's second most important festival, after the late September Festes de la Mercè/Fiestas de la Mercè.)

Even though the Festa Major de Gràcia is a neighborhood event, people from all the other neighborhoods of Barcelona stream into Gràcia for the event. Each street in the neighborhood vies for the prize for creating the most original street decorations. Many streets and plazas have their own designated bands or orchestras, people dance in the streets, and tables are set outdoors for partaking in an excess of fine foods and drink.

While much of Barcelona piles into Gràcia for this great event, some Gràcia residents along with a significant number of people from other neighborhoods empty out of the city, in search of peace and tranquility. They flee to Costa Brava beach towns or ancient mountain villages. So in effect, in August during the Festa Major de Gràcia, the traffic of humanity flows in two opposite directions, representing two opposite persuasions regarding the nurturing of psychological time: winding up for frenetic festivities or winding down on the beach and in the mountains.

ACCEPTING THE INEVITABLE

One could lead a joyous life in the Barcelona region without attending any of the numerous festivals or fairs. But never missing a dance is an attractive alternative. Our strategy sought a middle ground. We decided to live as if no annual revelry were taking place, letting destiny place us in the lap of whichever festivals were in our path. Without ever consulting a calendar of festivals, we found ourselves swept up by the crowd at the 24 September Festes de la Mercè, joining the *gegants*, giant figures representing religious and historical characters that tower over the throngs. And we couldn't help but get caught up by the eve of 24 June Día de Sant Joan/Día de San Juan, with its drinking, dancing and fireworks.

This laissez-faire festivalism outdid the guidebook itinerary. A random street poster, for example, led us to a memorable peak experience: a 24-hour non-stop blues festival that wasn't even listed in *Lonely Planet*. When a guitarist got tired, he left the stage and another guitarist jumped in to take his place. Sax players were abundant, taking turns on the stage. The band metamorphosed, and the music reached new depths of emotion with each fortuitous combo. This was one of the festivals we found. But with this strategy, we'll never know what we missed.

Other strategies can be considered. There's the qualitative approach: remain in your neighborhood, get involved with organizing committees, and have a deeper and more humanizing festival experience. Within any given neighborhood you'll have more than enough festivals to fill a calendar year.

179

Then there's the strategy of alternation: jive it up at a hedonistic festival and then repent at a religious one, although it's not as simple as it seems, since some religious festivals can get pretty hedonistic.

The eating-and-dancing strategy gets a positive rating, since you can eat all you want and then dance off the calories.

The eclectic fair-going strategy is an alternative to partying in the street. At the Fira de Barcelona/Feria de Barcelona (Av. Diagonal, 452-454), you can develop your multiple personalities. Become a peeping tom at the Intimate Apparel Salon in January/February, create your own gourmet buffet at the International Salon of Food and Drink in March, and consider time travel at the Exposition of Collectible Automobiles and Motorcycles in October/November.

The period covering June through October contains the most intense and unpredictable array of festivals, including every imaginable type of music. Culture is expensive in Barcelona, but during this period, you can hear some of the same musicians for free in park and street concerts.

An annotated addenda of the more important or unusual annual events is listed for handy reference. To find out what's the next festival, phone the city's primary organizers:

Institut de Cultura de Barcelona (CUB): 93 301 77 75
Institut Municipal de Parcs i Jardins: 93 424 38 09

Other organizer numbers are listed within the calendar. Some of the most bizarre neighborhood festivals are not widely publicized. There are, for example, the crowds of children and adults in their child mode throwing candy at horseback riders at Gràcia's Sant Medín festival, leaving the streets gummy and gooey for days. Word of mouth is the best source for such alternative neighborhood festivals.

JANUARY

Cavalcada dels Reis. 5 January. Los Reyes Magos, the three kings, the three wise men: for Barcelona children and adults as well, these are the ones who do the job of Santa Claus, with much more symbolic authenticity. The Institut de Cultura de Barcelona organizes a parade with floats, and the three kings spread goodwill the day before they bring gifts.

FEBRUARY

Carnaval. Two end-of-February festivals are equivalent to the "carnaval" that Brazil and New Orleans have cultivated. Carnestoltes lasts for nearly two weeks and ends on the traditional Tuesday known throughout Spain as "Martes del Carnaval", a month and a half before Easter. Also, Festes de Santa Eulalia, a more cultural version, concerts, parade of dragons. City Hall is the sponsor.

MARCH

Holy Week, end of March and/or April, including an elaborate Good Friday procession. Throughout the Hispanic world, "Semana Santa" is an official holiday, and many people take advantage and leave town for a vacation. Religious fraternities (*cofradías*) and penitents participate in the parade, taking a towering version of the Virgin Mary through the heart of the tourist district. But this is no show. It's an impressive exhibition of faith.

APRIL

Holy Week.
Día de Sant Jordi/Book Fair. 23 April. Kiosks of books and flowers on Las Ramblas and Plaça de Sant Jaume. New spring book titles are published.

MAY

Jazz a l'Hivernacle, May through September, organized by the Municipal Institute of Parks and Gardens, in the Hivernacle Auditorium, Parc de la Ciutadella.

JUNE

Summer "Grec" Festival, organized by the Institut de Cultura de Barcelona. June through August. Theater, dance and other performing arts. Various venues. Tickets sold wherever the Office de Tourisme sign appears.

Día de Sant Joan. 24 June, and the prior eve. Summer solstice. Fireworks, special pastries, dancing, drinking. Also called Night of Fire, our son's favorite festival thanks to the participatory fireworks that erupt in every neighborhood. The safest and most spectacular view of this festival is from afar, from a yacht or suburban balcony looking down on the city. Both the official fireworks experts and unofficial pyrotechnical champions light the sky.

Classica als Parcs, a series of classical music concerts in parks throughout the city.

Jazz a l'Hivernacle continues.

Gay-Lesbian Parade and Festival, end of June. Call Casal Lambda, 93 412 72 72, for information on this and later theater and film festivals with gay-lesbian themes.

JULY

Grec Festival continues.
Classica als Parcs continues.
Jazz a l'Hivernacle continues.

AUGUST

Jazz a l'Hivernacle continues.

Daniel Giordano Leis

Eating and dancing it off (overleaf) at Festa Major de Gràcia.

Grec Festival continues.

Festa Major de Gràcia, around August 15. One of the most exuberant neighborhood festivals, street decorating competition, bands and orchestras of every genre, including straight-ahead jazz in the intimate plazas, community feasting, drinking and lots of dancing. (Phone: 93 291 66 00)

Another neighborhood festival is Festa Major de Sants (August 24).

SEPTEMBER

La Diada Nacional. 11 September. Unlike July 4 in the United States or July 14 in France, Catalonia's national day commemorates a defeat rather than a victory, when the Generalitat finally succumbed to the Spaniards in 1714 after 18 months of heroic resistance. Some of those who still believe in independence for Catalonia will make themselves seen and heard on this day.

183

Ajuntament de Barcelona

Els Gegants

Festes de la Mercè. 24 September, for a week. Our Lady of the Mercè, patron saint and protectress of Barcelona. This is *the* festival of Barcelona. Includes competitive events such as a marathon, a swimming race, free concerts downtown and on the beachfront sponsored by Barcelona Acció Musical, and a rich variety of both indoor and outdoor cultural events, including the ubiquitous *sardanas* and giant figures holding their impressively designed heads far above the crowd. People literally play with fire, and safety experts won't recommend your involvement in ceremonial pyres. When it begins to get too hot, jump into a cultural event in any nearby art gallery.

Festa Major de la Barceloneta, another neighborhood festival. La Barceloneta, with its straight and narrow streets and laundry draping to dry over wrought-iron balconies, is the seaport community of Barcelona, and a great place to party and have seafood. Check posters for dates.

Jazz a l'Hivernacle continues.

185

OCTOBER

International Jazz Festival (call Music Project, 93 232 61 67, for dates)

Festival de Músiques del Món de Barcelona (World Music Festival, phone Fundación la Caixa: 93 207 74 75).

Festa Major de la Barceloneta continues.

Twentieth Century Music Festival, Mercat de les Flors Auditorium.

NOVEMBER

Twentieth Century Music Festival continues.

DECEMBER

Santa Llucia Christmas Fair. Districte de Ciutat Vella, phone 93 291 61 00 for information.

Christmas/Nadal/Navidad. Elaborate Nativity scenes are displayed in the main plazas, especially Plaça de Sant Jaume. Look carefully at the statuettes in these Nativity scenes and you'll pick out unique Catalan intruders, called the *caganers* ("shitters"), little men in a hut, doing their necessities. None of my Catalan friends could tell me the origins of this local insertion in the Nativity scenes.

Tip! *Els Castells*

Els Castells are human castles in which acrobatic and agile athletes, *els castellers*, are held on each other's shoulders to make a human castle. The *castells* is considered an amateur sport, but you're most likely to find them at any number of *festes majors* or *fiestas mayores*. So as to not miss this competition, when attending a fiesta, be sure to ask: if, where and when the *castellers* will be presenting their act. These human towers may reach as high as nine "floors" and the art and sport of creating the castle includes the skill of dismantling it.

Ajuntament de Barcelona

The castellers, human pyramids, at Festes de la Mercè.

The custom originated during the late nineteenth century, when it was an all-male activity. Today, you may find women participating as well.

In the *castells* competition, various teams compete to see which one "builds" the best human castle. These competitions are more likely to be found in the south of Catalonia but we've seen them in Barcelona as well. In fact, the *castellers* also travel to other countries to compete, and the Catalan community in Paris has invited them for important festival dates.

BIBLIOGRAPHY

Aroca, Montse Sanchez. "Voices inside schools: La Vemeda-Sant Martí: a school where people dare to dream. *Harvard Educational Review*, Fall 1999, 320–335.

Bohigas, Oriol. "Ten Points for an Urban Methodology," *Architectural Review* (Sep 1999, 88–91).

Foreign Investment in the Barcelona Area: a survey of foreign entrepreneurs in Barcelona by the Barcelona City Hall and KPMG Consulting.

Guiter, Henri. *Proverbes et Dictons Catalans*, bilingual edition, French/Catalan. Robert Morel Editeur, Paris, 1969.

Investing in Barcelona. Barcelona City Council: Barcelona, 2000.

Mendoza, Eduardo. *La Ciudad de los Prodigios*. Barcelona: Editorial Seix Barral, 1986. Ambitious historical novel whose sense of place and cultural implications serve as a visceral introduction to Barcelona.

Mendoza, Eduardo. *Sin Noticias de Gurb*. Barcelona: Editorial Seix Barral, 1991. Two extraterrestrials are on a mission to earth, in Barcelona. As long as we don't take everything literally, reading how Gurb and his partner-narrator adjust to Barcelona will help us in our own adjustment.

Michener, James A. *Iberia: Spanish Travels and Reflections*, "Barcelona," 540–621. New York: Random House, 1968. Michener's descriptions of the folk dance, *La Sardana*, the Las Ramblas boulevard, and Montserrat, plus his capturing of opinions on Catalonia's regional identity remain valid today.

Musseau, François, "Le Roi Pujol Vacille", *Le Point*, 8 Oct 1999, 76–79. An in-depth look at the historical rivalry between the conservative nationalist Jordi Pujol and the social democrat Pasqual Maragall.

Orwell, George. *Homage to Catalonia*. Middlesex, England: Penguin Books, 1962. First published in 1938. Orwell fought as a volunteer

189

on the leftist Republican side in the Spanish Civil War in 1937. Orwell was based in Barcelona. His on-site analysis of this crucial moment in the history of Catalunya is a dramatic way for the reader to get a feel for the social dynamics of the Barcelona of the time, whose indelible imprint can help explain contemporary thought and customs.

Pla, Josep. Catalan master of prose Josep Pla has made a sensorial art of the combination of travel writing and storytelling. Some of his works have become objective historical documents, such as his 1925 essays on his trip to Russia. A reading of Pla's stories of the Costa Brava (a favorite weekend retreat of Barcelona residents) will enhance one's visit to that region. Pla's *Històries de Cada Dia*, Barcelona: Llibres a Ma, 1989, collects stories from seven of Pla's books, which take place in various parts of Catalonia, including Barcelona. Pla is revered by proud Catalans for having defended their language with his writing when it was under siege.

Reflexions sobre Barcelona, the transcript of a 1991 Barcelona forum of urbanologists, in Catalan. Barcelona: Tibidabo Edicions, 1991. Barcelona's quality of life is discussed from the points of view of physical layout and municipal functions.

Relaciones de las culturas castellana y catalana: a Forum of Intellectuals, December 20–22, 1981. Barcelona: Generalitat de Catalunya, 1983. This primary source is the transcript of a historical encounter between Catalan and Castillian intellectuals, in which, with great honesty but also with an abundance of civility, representatives from these two cultures hash out their differences and seek a common ground. All the nuances of Catalan cultural nationalism emerge in these sometimes sensitive, other times dramatic exchanges of opinion.

[Polemics on the balance or imbalance between the Catalan and Spanish languages in Catalonia continue through contemporary times, as illustrated by numerous recent articles. A few are cited here: Letter-to-the-editor page in France's *L'Express* ("Ne tirez sur le catalan", literally, "Don't shoot against Catalan", 18 Nov 1999, p. 11) in reaction to an anti-nationalist feature article in the 14 October 1999 issue of

L'Express, "Catalogne: les décus du nationalisme" ("Catalonia: the Disappointment of Nationalism").

Politician Josep Lluís Carod-Rovira engaged in similar polemics during the October 1999 electoral campaign in a 12 October 1999 *La Vanguardia* interview entitled "Identificar la política lingüística con la cultural ha llevado a gestionar mal las dos" ("Identifying linguistic politics with cultural politics has led to bad results for both"). A bibliography on the debates on the Catalan language and its relationship of power or weakness with "Castillian" would easily fill a whole volume.]

Routes into Catalonia's Ancient Past, Generalitat de Catalunya, Departament d'Industria, Comerç i Turisme.

Rutas del Patrimonio Industrial, Generalitat de Catalunya, Departament d'Industria, Comerç i Turisme.

Roig, Montserrat and Goetzinger, Annie. *Mémoires de Barcelone*. Paris: Editions La Sirene, 1993. Catalan novelist and essayist Montserrat Roig and artist and writer Annie Goetzinger commemorate their friendship by integrating the essays of Roig with Goetzinger's drawings and poetic captions of Barcelona, a way the two could enjoy one last promenade through Barcelona before Roig's premature death from cancer. A beautiful book with much understated wisdom.

Vásquez Montalbán, Manuel. Within his novels and essays, most of them originally in Spanish, one finds exquisite insights and nuances about his native Barcelona. Within a French guide called *Barcelone: Un Guide Intime: avec M. Vásquez Montalbán*, Paris: Autrement Editions, 1987 is an elegant Vásquez Montalbán essay in French, "Résurgences de villes enfouies," in which the author offers a unique tactile, historical vision of his city, still valid today. In 13 pages, with haiku style precision, he captures the essence of the history and heartbeat of Barcelona.

Vásquez Montalbán, Manuel. *La Rosa de Alejandría*, Barcelona: Planeta, 1984. Good story, great recipes, starring the gourmet private eye Pepe Carvalho.

THE AUTHOR

Mark Cramer has lived in New York, California, Mexico City, Barcelona, La Paz (Bolivia), and Paris, among other places, with frequent trips to Havana. But he's not a drifter, and believes in establishing roots wherever he goes. His Culture Shock! books on these places have been well-received by the sternest local observers.

He currently lives with his wife and son in the 20th Arrondissement of Paris. His son is the only American in his school ("American" from both his U.S. and Bolivian heritage).

His *FunkyTowns USA: the Best Alternative, Eclectic and Visionary Places* was featured on CNN and written up in more than 50 newspapers and journals, and is used as an "underground" text in several universities. Author and urbanologist Ray Oldenburg calls Cramer "a seasoned expert in urban anatomy."

When he's not writing, Cramer is hiking, listening to jazz, reading Charles Bukowski, studying the racing form, or hanging out for hours at the friendliest neighborhood cafe-bar in an attempt to slow down the clock.

INDEX

Praise for other books written by Mark Cramer:

Living & Working Abroad: New York

"*Living & Working Abroad: New York* is a bit of philosophy, a bit of sociology, and a lot of very practical and helpful information. The reader experiences the nitty-gritty of daily life in New York, from 'Should I have a car?' to 'How can I start a business?' to 'Can I afford to buy a house?' and much, much more. Don't venture into the city without it."

—Cy Yoakam, Editor of *Urban Quality Indicators*

Culture Shock! Bolivia

"Many South American travel guides are simply exhaustive tomes of statistics, histories and tips, failed attempts to intimately cover all the bases. These books are for the stereotypical traveler who wants to skirt all the main tourist stops and go home ... Maybe they should take a few tips from Mark Cramer, author of *Culture Shock! Bolivia*. The book culls the most provocative, juiciest aspects of the country ... Cramer has been able to submerge himself deep into Bolivian culture and current events, to discover the country's disparate attractions and reveal the catalytic even shaped today's Bolivia."

— Erik Loza, *Bolivian Times*

Culture Shock! Cuba

"I really thought *Culture Shock! Cuba* was informative and helpful. I will have my students buy it for their trip to Cuba."

—Professor Jon Torgerson, Department of Philosophy and Religion, Drake University

"The book is terrific."

—John S. Kavulich II, President, US-Cuba Trade and Economic Council Inc.